THE LIBRARY OF MEDIEVAL TIMES

Medieval Punishment and Torture

Stephen Currie

ReferencePoint Press®

San Diego, CA

ReferencePoint Press®

Printed in the United States

For more information, contact:
ReferencePoint Press, Inc.
PO Box 27779
San Diego, CA 92198
www. ReferencePointPress.com

LIBRARY OF CONGRESS CATALOGING-IN-PUBLICATION DATA

Currie, Stephen, 1960-
Medieval punishment and torture / by Stephen Currie.
pages cm. -- (The library of Medieval times)
Includes bibliographical references and index.
ISBN-13: 978-1-60152-658-8 (hardback)
ISBN-10: 1-60152-658-X (hardback)
1. Punishment--Europe--History--To 1500--Juvenile literature. 2. Torture--Europe--History--To 1500--Juvenile literature. 3. Crime--Europe--History--To 1500--Juvenile literature 4. Europe--History--476-1492--Juvenile literature. I. Title.
HV8532.E85C87 2015
364.6094'0902--dc23

2013045389

CONTENTS

Important Events of Medieval Times 4

Introduction 6
The Middle Ages and Torture

Chapter One 10
Crime in the Middle Ages

Chapter Two 21
Ordeals and Confessions

Chapter Three 32
Medieval Prisons

Chapter Four 44
Tortures and Torments

Chapter Five 57
Capital Punishment

Source Notes 69

For Further Research 72

Index 74

Picture Credits 79

About the Author 80

IMPORTANT EVENTS OF MEDIEVAL TIMES

400 | 600 | 800 | 1000 | 1200

476
Romulus Augustulus, the last Roman emperor in the West, is dethroned.

632
The Prophet Muhammad dies as Islam begins to expand both east and west of the Arabian Peninsula.

800
In Rome, Pope Leo III crowns Charlemagne emperor; his Carolingian dynasty rules western Europe until 987.

ca. 950
Europe's first medical school opens in Salerno, Italy.

1000
A century of invention in farming begins; devices such as the heavy plow increase agricultural productivity and help double Europe's population.

1066
William of Normandy defeats the last Anglo-Saxon king at the Battle of Hastings, establishing Norman rule in England.

1099
The First Crusade ends Muslim rule in Jerusalem until 1187, when the Muslims under Saladin recapture Jerusalem from the Crusaders.

1130
Church authorities in France ban tournaments; the ban on these popular festivals, which provide knights with opportunities to gain prestige and financial reward, is later reversed.

1184
Church officials meeting in Verona, Italy, approve burning at the stake as a punishment for anyone found guilty of heresy.

1200
The rise of universities begins to promote a revival of learning throughout the West.

1215
King John of England signs the Magna Carta, limiting the rights of the monarchy.

1231
Pope Gregory IX establishes the "Holy Inquisition," whose purpose is to search out heretics and force them to renounce their views.

1267
Henry III of England enacts the Assize of Bread and Ale, one of the first laws to regulate the production and sale of food; the law ties the price of bread to the price of wheat, thus preventing bakers from setting artificially high prices.

1316
The Italian physician Mondino De' Luzzi writes the first book of the medieval period devoted entirely to anatomy.

1328
Charles IV dies, ending 341 years of successful rule by the Capetian kings who established modern France.

1337
The Hundred Years' War begins between France and England.

1346
Using the longbow, English archers overwhelm the French army at the Battle of Crécy during the Hundred Years' War.

1347
The deadly bubonic plague strikes Europe and returns intermittently for the next 250 years.

1378
The Great Schism, in which there are three claimants to the papacy, occurs.

1453
The Ottoman Turks conquer Constantinople following a seven-week bombardment with cannons.

1250 1300 1350 1400 1450

INTRODUCTION

The Middle Ages and Torture

In 1307 a group of knights known as the Templars caught the attention of Philip IV the Fair, king of France. Jealous of the Templars' power and wealth, Philip decided to use his influence to destroy the group altogether. Accordingly, Philip accused the Templars—individually and as a group—of a long list of trumped-up crimes that included sorcery, devil worship, and much more. When the Templars dismissed the allegations as completely untrue—which they were—Philip was prepared. Joining forces with Pope Clement V, he had the knights arrested and brutally tortured over a period of several weeks.

The tortures were grim indeed. The torturers beat the knights unmercifully, fracturing bones and damaging joints. They stretched the Templars' bodies on diabolical machines that dislocated shoulders and arms. They knocked out the knights' teeth and refused them food. At last, broken in both body and spirit, the men began admitting to the charges. Among those who confessed was the group's leader, Jacques DeMolay. Eager for the tortures to come to an end, DeMolay admitted that he and his fellow knights had denied the divinity of Jesus and had mocked the cross and other important symbols of Christianity. "And [DeMolay] would have confessed that he had slain God Himself," wrote an author who lived at the time, "if they had asked him that."[1]

Given the abuse to which DeMolay and his fellow knights were subjected, it is hard to blame them for admitting to crimes they did not commit. Indeed, after days of appalling violence, it would have taken an exceptionally strong person to continue to hold out when a confession, genuine or not, would have brought the torture to a close. Regardless of why DeMolay and the others had agreed to admit wrongdoing, Philip and Clement were delighted with the confessions. They had successfully discredited and dismantled the Templars and gained power at their expense.

The story was not over, however. With the tortures having run their course, DeMolay thought better of his confession. In 1309 he recanted his testimony—that is, he admitted that he had not told the truth. Furious, Philip sentenced DeMolay and many of his followers to death by burning—an especially horrifying method of capital punishment in which victims were tied to a post and forced to stand as their bodies were consumed by flames. In 1314 the sentence was carried out on DeMolay. It was a dreadful end for a man who had never committed any sort of crime whatsoever.

WORDS IN CONTEXT

recant: Take back testimony.

"The Stuff of Nightmares"

The experiences of DeMolay and his fellow Templars, though, were hardly unusual for medieval Europeans. Throughout the Middle Ages, which stretched from the 400s to the 1300s and perhaps beyond, many tens of thousands of people lost their lives through grim and terrible measures, often for crimes they had never committed. Millions more, in turn, were brutally tortured, their bodies twisted and torn in grotesque ways which as often as not resulted in permanent damage. Once again, many of the people thus victimized were completely innocent, and even those who were guilty had often committed a crime no more serious than petty theft.

Though overshadowed by the classical era, which preceded it, and the Renaissance, which followed it, medieval Europe has long been known for creativity in architecture, literature, music, and other important aspects of culture. Unfortunately, the creativity that medieval Europeans poured into art, poetry, and technology was accompanied by

another—and much more appalling—form of inventiveness: torture and punishment. Many medieval punishments were designed to cause the maximum possible pain, and the Europeans of the time had ample opportunity to practice their craft on living, breathing human beings. The torture devices of the Middle Ages, writes a modern historian, were "the stuff of nightmares."[2]

Indeed, compassion was not a much-admired virtue during the Middle Ages in dealing with prisoners and criminals. To be sure, a few medieval voices urged those in power to err on the side of mercy. In 1162, for instance, Pope Alexander III noted that it was "better to pardon the guilty than to take the lives of the innocent"[3]—a guiding principle that seems basic to modern Americans but was unusual for the medieval period. Much more in tune with the spirit of the times was a high-ranking Church official a generation or so later who recommended slaughtering thousands of people in a French town, only some of whom were believed to be criminals. "Kill them all," the man is supposed to have said. "The Lord knows those who are his own."[4]

WORDS IN CONTEXT

ruthlessness: Cruelty, lack of mercy.

Whatever they were charged with, the medieval Europeans who ran afoul of the law were not to be envied. They were subjected to some of the most gruesome and painful punishments ever devised by the human mind. Medieval Europe was by no means the only society in world history that used brutal tortures, nor was it the only one to use the death penalty. But more than many other societies through time, the medieval period was defined in part by the ruthlessness of the tortures and punishments its people created and carried out—all too often on the innocent as well as on the guilty. Sadly, this heritage of torture and cruelty remains one of the best-known legacies of the medieval era.

CHAPTER ONE

Crime in the Middle Ages

It was easy to run afoul of the law during the Middle Ages. Millions of medieval Europeans were arrested and tried for violent crimes such as murder and property crimes like theft. The medieval era had plenty of religious laws, too, and breaking them led to penalties at least as significant as those that punished arson or armed robbery. And in a world where the nobility often ruled as dictators, crimes were frequently invented to suit the desires of those in power. There were many medieval leaders such as Bernabo, an Italian ruler of the 1300s who criminalized almost any activity he did not like—including the mistreatment of his animals. "If any of his 500 hunting dogs was not in good condition," writes historian Barbara Tuchman, "he would have the keepers hanged."[5]

Violent Crime

Crime, especially violent crime, was widespread during the Middle Ages. By modern standards the medieval period was exceptionally bloody, with a myriad of wars and a strong code of honor that often led men and armies to fight. As a result, battery, robbery, murder, and other violent offenses were frequent. Murder, for example, was at least five times more common during the medieval era than it is today. Some of these murders were premeditated, but the majority were carried out in the heat of the moment. "Most homicides took place during an argument or brawl," writes historian Joyce Lee Malcolm. "Weapons used in killings in hot blood tended to be items near at hand—tools, sticks and stones, or simply hands and feet."[6]

Other crimes of violence were part of everyday life as well. Even if a brawl did not end in death, it often caused significant injuries to one or more of the combatants. Stab wounds, knocked-out teeth, and broken bones were especially frequent outcomes. Armed robbery was common, too, with travelers particularly susceptible. Highwaymen with swords and clubs concealed themselves along roads and attacked passersby, taking their valuables and frequently leaving the unfortunate travelers near death. However, armed robbery was hardly unusual away from the roads either. In 1202 the small English town of Lincoln recorded eighty-nine violent robberies—an enormous number given that the population of the town probably did not exceed three thousand.

WORDS IN CONTEXT

arson: Deliberate setting of a fire.

Rape, another crime of violence, was specifically forbidden by many medieval societies. "Rape is a felony committed by a man by violence on the body of a woman, whether she be a virgin or not,"[7] reads an English law of the 1200s. The evidence suggests, however, that rape was rarely punished. Women had a difficult time proving that they had been raped, and the male-dominated courts of the time were not inclined to convict accused rapists unless significant violence accompanied the rape. The result was that many women never reported assaults. One French community recorded an average of about two rapes a month in the 1300s, but most scholars believe that the actual figure was considerably more.

Burglary, Theft, and Debt

Property crimes such as burglary were a problem in the Middle Ages as well. Many medieval thieves were professionals. They made their living breaking into houses and stealing money; alternatively, they took valuable goods such as cloth or jewels, which they then pawned or resold. Often these criminals worked in groups. During the 1300s, for instance, an Italian man known as Maleta was widely known as the "captain, guide, and promoter of all the thieves"[8] in the area where he lived, and other communities had similar gangs with equally influential leaders.

Theft in the Middle Ages, however, was by no means the sole province of experts. Many normally law-abiding Europeans of the medieval period stole when they thought they could get away with it. Sometimes the motivation was greed. More often, though, the theft was out of necessity. Most medieval Europeans lived in extreme poverty and seldom had enough to eat. Faced with a choice of starving to death or surviving by stealing, most desperately poor peasants elected the latter. Some took money to buy food and other essentials. Others took food directly, stealing a loaf of bread, a bag of grain, or some fruit from a neighbor fortunate enough to have a decent food supply.

Debt was another crime common during the medieval era. Being unable to repay money owed to someone else was considered a very serious offense, and debtors were subject to a variety of punishments, many of them quite serious. Debt affected people on most social and economic levels of the medieval era. Merchants, for example, might buy a wagonload of goods on credit in the expectation of being able to sell it later on for a profit, only to discover that economic depression or simple misreading of the market made it impossible to repay the debt. Villagers, similarly, were often forced to borrow to obtain the basic necessities of life, and nobles frequently borrowed to keep up appearances.

More Laws

Not all medieval crimes were directly related to violence, property, or economics. One often-prosecuted crime during the Middle Ages, for example, was known as vagrancy. It consisted of wandering from one place to another without having a job or permanent place of residence. Many vagrants were beggars unable or unwilling to work and driven from one town to another. Many others were ill with communicable diseases such as leprosy, a condition characterized by skin sores, damage to the nerves, and disfigurement. Few medieval communities wanted lepers living among them, so they were often charged with vagrancy if they failed to move on in a timely manner. Whether aimed at beggars

Two peasants, desperate for food, fill a bag with stolen wheat. Faced with the choice of stealing or starving to death, most impoverished people of the Middle Ages chose theft despite severe consequences if caught.

or lepers, vagrancy laws were used to keep unwanted people away from towns and villages.

Mounting a challenge to the authority of nobles and monarchs was treason, which was also a crime. Europe in the Middle Ages was a hotbed of political intrigue, with nobles often plotting to overthrow other, more powerful lords. Taking part in a rebellion against a lord was a punishable offense, assuming that the lord remained in power long enough to actually penalize the offenders. In 1174, for example, Scottish nobleman William the Lion was one of many people imprisoned for staging an unsuccessful revolt against England's King Henry II. Commoners could run afoul of these laws as well. In 1381 about twenty thousand English peasants revolted against King Richard II. For a time it appeared possible that the rebels would succeed: "So shall we be lords of all the realm without doubt,"[9] rebel leader Wat Tyler is supposed to have said. But in the end Tyler and his fellow leaders were captured and charged with treason.

WORDS IN CONTEXT

treason: Challenging the authority of a leader or state.

The law covered other activities as well. Many women in medieval Europe were arrested for being scolds, a term defined by a modern historian as "a troublesome and angry woman who, by brawling and wrangling amongst her neighbours, breaks the public peace, increases discord and becomes a public nuisance."[10] Fistfights among men were against the law, too, but unlike women, men would be arrested not for being scolds but for disturbing the peace. Those receiving stolen goods were likewise breaking the law. So were people who criticized the king or an important lord, even if they did not take part in armed revolt; such criticisms were considered another form of treason. All these doings and many more were crimes in the Middle Ages—and all were worthy of some kind of punishment.

Witchcraft

The crimes of violence and crimes against property common during the Middle Ages are generally familiar to North Americans today. The medieval era, however, did judge some activities as crimes that are no longer viewed that way in Western society. Foremost among these was witchcraft. The Christians of the medieval period accepted the existence of the devil, known as Satan. The theology of the time viewed God and Satan as locked in an eternal struggle for control of the universe. Satan was believed to be extremely active in the ordinary workings of the world, routinely disguising himself to make appearances on Earth in an attempt to convince Christians to join his side. Those who let down their guard, even for an instant, could be claimed by the forces of evil. In the Middle Ages, those who

Coin Clipping

The medieval economy relied on barter, or the exchange of goods, more than on a monetary system. Still, money did exist, and many European governments issued coins. The value of each coin was based entirely on the value of the metal it contained. A gold coin was worth more than a silver coin of the same size, for example, and larger coins of any given material were worth more than smaller ones made from the same metal. Each government attempted to standardize the sizes and metals of each coin. Thus, any large copper coin, say, might be expected to contain a shilling's worth of metal, while a small gold coin might be ten or twelve times as valuable.

Enterprising Europeans, however, discovered that they could clip the coins, or shave metal from them without significantly changing the way they looked. An unsuspecting merchant or debtor would accept the coin at full value, only to discover later on that the smaller amount of metal made it actually worth less. The coin clipper, in turn, would melt down the shaved metal and sell it for its actual value.

Coin clipping diminished trust in the European monetary system, defrauded innocent victims, and brought the perpetrators income they did not earn. For all these reasons, coin clipping was against the law, and arrests for this offense during the medieval period were common. In 1278, for example, Edward I of England arrested six hundred people in a single day on charges of clipping coins.

were in league with the devil were known as witches, wizards, or sorcerers, and witchcraft was among the most serious of crimes. Wizardry, read one edict of the 700s, was "the very filth of the wicked."[11]

The people of the Middle Ages believed that witches led a double life. By day they could seem much like any ordinary villager or peasant. By night, however, they attended wild revels at which Satan himself often appeared. In the popular imagination, these celebrations were bacchanalian orgies filled with indiscriminate sex, the eating of babies, and a total contempt for religion and morality. The party lasted until the early hours of the morning, when the witches returned home ready to begin another day in human form. Some accused witches confirmed these tales, though generally under threat of torture if not during torture itself. In 1275, for instance, Frenchwoman Angela de la Barthe admitted to having had sex with the devil at one of these revels, later producing a child that was part snake and part wolf.

From a scientific and logical perspective, of course, these stories were full of contradictions, from the impossibility of snake-wolf offspring to the lack of time available for traveling to nighttime festivities. Such impossibilities, however, bothered few people of the Middle Ages. In a world where the existence of black magic was widely accepted, it seemed apparent that no earthly rules could stop the witches from doing as they pleased. Armed with powers given them by Satan himself, witches could travel distances in the blink of an eye, using what one historian sarcastically refers to as "broomsticks or spindles or airborne goats."[12] Even locking witches in a room or a dungeon might do no good; they had the ability to slide their bodies through keyholes or under doors.

Finding a Witch

For the people of the Middle Ages, moreover, witchcraft was a convenient explanation for practically anything that went wrong. An unseasonable snap of cold weather, killing crops in the field, was probably the result of a spell cast by a witch. The birth of a deformed child indicated the presence of sorcery; an epidemic, such as the Black Death that swept through western Europe in the mid-1300s, was almost certainly caused at least in part by witches. Unfortunately, because witches so often led a double life, finding those who caused the problems could be difficult. According to popular belief, witches could be identified by a spot on the body, the so-called devil's mark that was insensitive to pain. Moreover, witches often had familiars, black cats and other animals that helped Satan's minions in their quest to replace good with evil.

Even so, identifying a witch was more difficult than identifying a murderer, a vagrant, or a debtor, and authorities during the Middle Ages spent much time determining who was guilty of witchcraft. Most commonly, that meant asking people to identify neighbors they suspected of sorcery. Many people were very happy to oblige, often seizing the opportunity to report those they did not like or had been feuding with. The result was a series of unreliable accusations, nearly all of which were believed by credulous officials. "Suspected witches were routinely put on trial," notes a modern historian, writing of the later Middle Ages, "always with the presumption that they were guilty."[13]

In an effort to save their own skins, some of the accused immediately cast blame on others. This rarely helped their own cases, but it did lead to a domino effect in which half a village might eventually come under suspicion. Across Europe, historians estimate, hundreds of thousands of

An accused witch is subjected to the ducking stool. Drowning in water blessed by a priest proved innocence; not drowning proved guilt, which then led to being burned at the stake.

Sanctuary

One of the oddest aspects of medieval justice was the tradition of sanctuary, a system which allowed certain criminals to exchange a possible severe penalty for a somewhat lesser one. A sanctuary is a refuge; the word is often used to refer to a sacred place. By entering a church, suspected criminals could under some circumstances prevent secular authorities from arresting them. As long as they remained in the building and accepted an alternate punishment from Church officials, they were safe.

The alternate punishment was often better than going through the tortures or long-term imprisonment that secular authorities might mete out. Even so, it was far from pleasant. "The fugitive had to confess his misdeeds [to a priest], surrender his weapons, and ring the church bells," write historians Frances Gies and Joseph Gies, explaining the standard penalty. "The royal coroner came, heard his oath to abjure the realm [leave the country] forever, assigned him a port or border town by which to depart, and saw him branded on the thumb." The brand was permanent and served to alert others that the person had run afoul of the law.

The right of sanctuary was not absolute. It could only be used once in a lifetime. Nor was it available to certain classes of criminals, notably those who had committed especially serious crimes. Witches and traitors could not claim sanctuary, for example. But many thieves, arsonists, and petty criminals of the Middle Ages made use of this loophole to evade more serious punishment.

Frances and Joseph Gies, *Daily Life in Medieval Times.* New York: Black Dog and Leventhal, 1990, p. 218.

people were charged with witchcraft at one point or another during the medieval period. In the first half of the 1300s, for instance, officials in two French towns alone prosecuted a thousand people for witchcraft. Though it never actually existed, witchcraft was among the most widespread crimes of the Middle Ages.

Witchcraft was a crime both in the secular, or nonreligious, world of medieval Europe and in the religious sphere as well. The western Christian Church, which dominated the religious life of the Middle Ages, was deeply concerned with witchcraft; since sorcery was focused on the devil it was by definition opposed to God. Thus, suspected witches could run afoul of secular authorities and be subject to arrest by soldiers loyal to kings and dukes, and they could also be arrested and tried by clerical courts. Indeed, the two legal systems often worked together, especially toward the end of the medieval period, to locate, arrest, and punish suspected witches.

WORDS IN CONTEXT

secular: Having to do with the world rather than with religion.

Heresy

Though witchcraft was of great interest to Church authorities during the medieval era, another crime was viewed by the Church as equally bad: heresy, or holding beliefs contrary to official Church teachings. As far as the Church was concerned, only one path led to salvation of the soul, and that was through the Church itself. Since heretics rejected the Church, they were therefore damned for all eternity. Church officials worried, however, that heretical ideas would spread quickly from one person or community to another. As a consequence, they worked hard to keep heresies from arising at all and came down enthusiastically on those who held heretical beliefs. "The heretics have lain concealed for a long time," observed Pope Gregory IX in 1231, "scuttling about in hiding like crabs."[14]

The details of heresy varied considerably. Some heretics denied that Jesus Christ was fully human as well as divine, as the Church taught. Others rejected the Church's view of the nature of evil. Regardless of the specifics, the Church responded ferociously to Christians who held different perspectives. For example, Church leaders often demonized the heretics by spreading misinformation about them that would place them in the worst possible light. A monk charged that one group of French heretics ceremonially ate food "made from the ashes of a murdered baby,"[15] for example, and a Church official described another dissident group as "the ministers of the Old Serpent [Satan]."[16]

Despite the disapproval of the Church, heretical thinking seemed to grow during the 1100s and into the 1200s. In the mid-1200s Church leaders increased their antiheresy vigilance by starting a campaign called the Inquisition. Described by historian Jonathan Kirsch as "a total war"[17] against heretical thinking, the Inquisition was carried out by clerics charged with rooting out heresies by any means necessary. These men were known as inquisitors, and they were given extraordinary powers to interrogate, arrest, and torture suspected heretics. The Inquisition led to the arrest of hundreds of thousands of people all over Europe on charges of heresy. As with witchcraft, inquisitors typically assumed that those who were accused of heresy were guilty. While some of the accused undoubtedly held heretical beliefs, many more did not; unfortunately, very few were found innocent.

WORDS IN CONTEXT

Inquisition: Organized effort to enforce orthodox thinking.

Crime of all varieties, then, was quite common during the medieval era. Treason and witchcraft, heresy and murder, vagrancy and petty theft: Whether real or imaginary, whether serious or minor, these and many other forms of misconduct were punishable offenses in the Middle Ages. Those unfortunate enough to be caught, tried, and found guilty of one of these crimes could generally expect a penalty both swift and harsh. The best strategy for a medieval European who wished to avoid the often violent punishments of the justice system was to avoid criminal behavior altogether. But as the overly wide nets cast for witches and heretics demonstrate, even staying away from criminal activity was no guarantee of remaining outside the justice system. In the end, whether a person was arrested or not depended as much on luck as on any other factor.

CHAPTER TWO

Ordeals and Confessions

There was no single overarching justice system in medieval Europe. On the contrary, dozens of different court systems prevailed from Sweden to Spain and from Italy to Ireland. Some medieval courts were ecclesiastical, or church-related, while others were secular. Some made use of jurors, with others run exclusively by judges. Some court systems answered to kings and queens who ruled entire countries, but others were set up by lesser nobles, such as earls and dukes, whose influence was more limited. Specific years played a role, too. As time went on courts gradually became more focused on written rules and laws, more likely to record information about cases, and more likely to inflict standardized punishments on the guilty.

All medieval courts were alike in three important ways, however. For one, they wielded great power. With no higher courts to hear a prisoner's appeal, their rulings were generally final. Second, they tended to punish people using methods that would strike modern Americans as astonishingly harsh. While a thief might be given a short prison term or required to pay a fine, for example, the possible punishments for such a crime might also include the amputation of a hand, the branding of the flesh, or even the death penalty. Heretics and scolds, thieves and witches—all were not only subject to torture but often made to suffer in ghastly ways that Westerners today would perceive as far out of proportion to the original crime.

Finally, the courts of the Middle Ages were alike in that they did not limit the use of tortures and other punishments to those who had been found guilty. Rather, they frequently subjected those who had not yet been found guilty to draconian punishment as well. That was especially true of prisoners who fell into one of two categories. The first category included those whose guilt or innocence could not easily be established through standard methods, such as eyewitness testimony or physical evidence. They were often put through tortures known as ordeals, which were designed to help authorities determine whether the prisoner should be found guilty. Ordeals were especially often used on people who were charged with nebulous crimes such as witchcraft and heresy; in such cases, determining culpability by normal methods was not always easy or even possible.

The second category included prisoners who had not yet confessed to criminal behavior. Courts, especially ecclesiastical courts, preferred to have prisoners confess to the crimes of which they had been accused. In many cases court officials were privately convinced that a suspect was guilty but were unable to get the suspect to admit his or her guilt. These suspects, too, were frequently victimized by brutal tortures until they were finally willing to confess. Grim as the tortures for convicted criminals could be, the tortures used on people in these other two categories could be equally appalling—and were in some ways worse since they were used on many people who in all probability were entirely innocent.

WORDS IN CONTEXT

ecclesiastical: Having to do with a church or religion.

Ordeals

Ordeals—the tortures used to determine a person's guilt or innocence—were based on a simple principle: The response of a suspected criminal to pain was directly correlated to the person's guilt. God, the theory ran, would intervene on behalf of those who were innocent, often producing a miracle to shield the truly blameless. There was biblical precedent for this. The Book of Numbers in the Hebrew bible, for instance, contains an ordeal-like test for determining whether a woman had committed

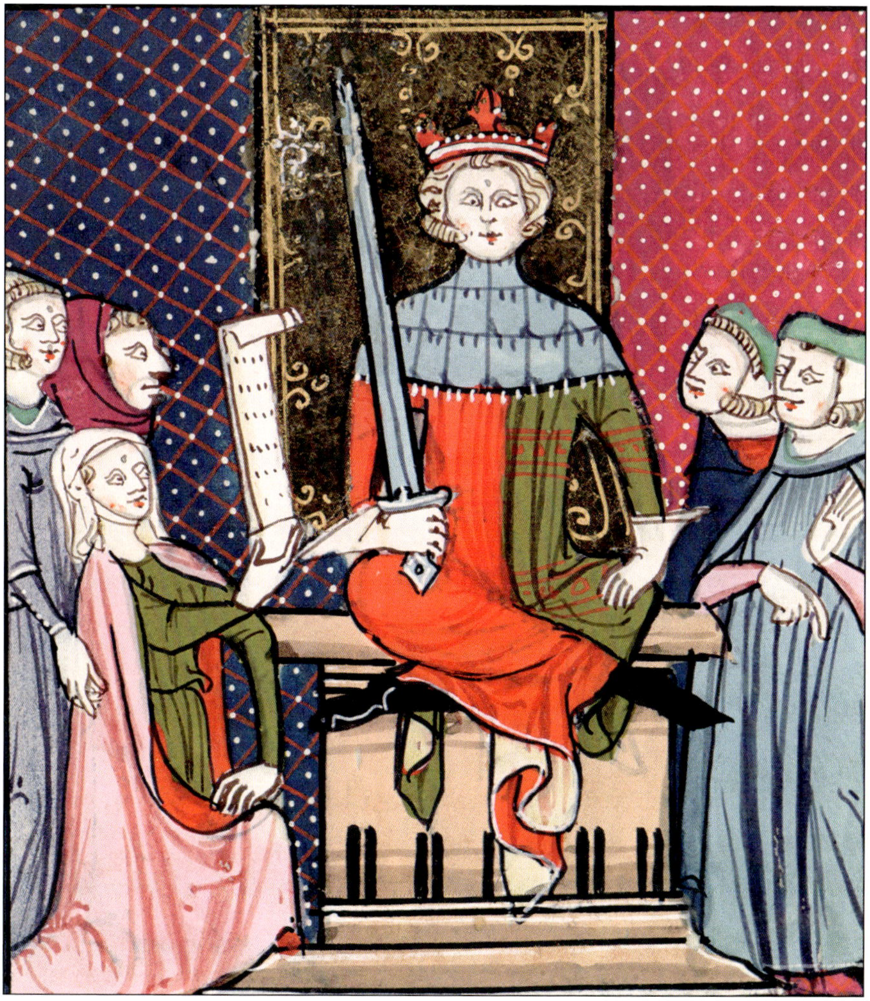

A woman accused of adultery appears in court to plead her case. In some instances, women accused of being unfaithful to their husbands were forced to undergo a test, or ordeal, that determined guilt or innocence.

adultery. In essence, the suspect would drink a mixture of holy water and dirt from the floor of a temple. If the combination made her sick, that was taken as evidence of her guilt. If she did not become ill, then she was declared innocent; God had protected her.

One excellent example of a medieval ordeal was the so-called ordeal by fire. In this torture the prisoner was restrained while a poker or other piece of iron was heated. Then the red-hot poker was held against the prisoner's flesh. In its most basic form, a prisoner whose skin miraculously showed no sign of charring or blistering would be declared innocent of all charges. In contrast, anyone whose skin was damaged by the poker—the great majority of those tested in this way—was presumed to be guilty and would be punished accordingly. Despite the odds against it, there were reports of individuals who managed to emerge unscathed from the ordeal by fire, thus proving their innocence. In the late 1000s, for instance, an English bishop who had been accused of treason against William the Conqueror escaped punishment after supposedly passing the poker test.

The ordeal by fire varied. Sometimes the flesh was bandaged immediately after being touched by the poker. Several days later the bindings were removed and the wound examined. If it had healed, which of course it usually had not, then the accused was innocent; whereas if the wound was healing slowly or not at all, that was taken as a sign of guilt. Ordeal by fire could also involve walking barefoot across a bed of fiery coals or metal. According to legend, eleventh-century Queen Cunigunde of Luxembourg was subjected to this ordeal when accused of adultery; because she walked across the coals without injury, she was assumed to be innocent. As with the poker, that outcome would have been highly unusual.

Ordeals by Water

Ordeal by water was another popular way of determining guilt. Like ordeal by fire, ordeal by water came in different forms. One type required a prisoner to thrust his or her bare arm into a cauldron of boiling water. If the flesh was unharmed, either immediately or after a period of three days, the prisoner was declared not guilty. Most of the time, however, the water badly burned the arm, causing intense pain and leading to a guilty verdict. Often this ordeal was carried out in a church, as a ritual that included holy water, priestly garments, and prayers. "Let the man who is to be tried, as well as the kettle or pot in which is the boiling water, be fumed with the incense of myrrh,"[18] read a formulary for carrying out the ordeal by water in religious surroundings.

Another variation on this practice was known as the Ordeal of Cold Water. This ordeal involved throwing a bound victim into a river or lake. If the victim was innocent, the water—a symbol of purity in Christianity—would "claim" the victim and cause the prisoner to sink. A guilty person, however, would be rejected by the water and would bob once again to the surface. Sometimes judges would assign a bystander to rescue a prisoner who sank, but it is not clear that this was always the case; moreover, a bystander could not be sure of getting the victim to the surface before the victim drowned. In any case, the ordeal brought great terror to those who underwent it, even if they were found not guilty.

WORDS IN CONTEXT

ordeals: Tests designed to determine guilt or innocence.

Ordeals were used frequently in the early years of the Middle Ages. By the 1200s, though, they were becoming less common. As medieval society became slightly more complex and sophisticated, people began to wonder whether passing an ordeal truly meant that a prisoner was innocent. Increasingly, it seemed that passing or failing an ordeal had more to do with random chance than with God's grace. Unfortunately, if there were no eyewitnesses to a crime, it was often impossible to build a case against a suspect. And that was doubly true for crimes such as heresy and sorcery, which were by nature secretive and carried out in private. The medieval justice system needed a replacement, and it found one in confession.

Confessing a Crime

Many legal codes of the later Middle Ages placed great value on confession. Although officials were almost always certain that a suspect was guilty before trying to extract a confession, it was useful to have some corroboration of this belief. In the absence of an eyewitness or physical evidence, a confession would usually suffice to ascertain a suspect's guilt. The confession, then, was more than just a formality. "The sweetest victory in the war on heresy," writes Jonathan Kirsch, was "a sincere and spontaneous admission of wrongdoing by the accused heretic"[19]—and the same applied to witches, murderers, thieves, and other potential lawbreakers as well.

Obtaining a Confession

Bernard Gui (1260–1331) was a French priest and inquisitor who is best known today for writing a book he called *On the Method, Practice, and Procedure Used in Seeking Out and Interrogating Heretics, Their Believers, and Accomplices.* This volume, also known by the shorter title *An Inquisitor's Manual,* served as a textbook for other inquisitors who hoped to get suspected heretics to confess their sins.

Gui was convinced that virtually all accused or suspected heretics were indeed guilty as charged, and his writing reflects that. He cautioned his readers that heretics would do whatever they could to conceal their guilt from others. "Because modern heretics endeavor and seek covertly to disguise their errors rather than openly to confess them," he wrote, "even men versed in the Scriptures cannot prove their guilt, because they manage to escape by verbal trickery and carefully contrived subtleties."

At the same time, Gui left no doubt that through proper questioning, a wise inquisitor could obtain a confession from even the most clever and determined of heretics. "With the bridle of discretion," he wrote, "let [the inquisitor] so harness the wiles of heretical persons that, with the help of God and the skill of a midwife, he may draw the writhing serpent from the sink and abyss of errors." It would be interesting to know how effective this questioning might have been had Gui and other inquisitors been forbidden to use physical and psychological pain to extract confessions from heretics and suspected heretics.

Quoted in Norman Cantor, *The Medieval Reader.* New York: HarperCollins, 1994, pp. 252–53.

With such a heavy emphasis on confession, it was understandable that medieval courts would go to great lengths to get a suspect to confess. All too often, that meant applying physical and psychological torture to the accused in an effort to obtain an admission of guilt. Indeed, the use of violence was strongly encouraged not only by secular authorities but by Church officials as well. "The official should obtain from all heretics he has captured a confession by torture,"[20] reads a mid-1200s directive from Pope Innocent IV. Under these circumstances, a suspected witch or heretic could expect to be tortured, often brutally, if he or she would not admit guilt right away—regardless of the validity of the charge. As a document of the late 1200s put it, the best way to "elicit the truth" in a criminal matter was through "torment and suffering of the body."[21]

To be sure, a few safeguards were in place. For instance, Innocent specified that torture should never lead to the death of the suspect. In some Belgian and Dutch towns during the late 1200s, similarly, torture required the approval of the town council. Moreover, in general, confessions obtained through torture were not admissible in court; the confession had to be repeated in a situation where the accused was not in fear of his or her life. In practice, however, these precautions did not always provide much protection. If the accused recanted, or took back the confession, after a session of being tortured, he or she would most likely be tortured again—and if necessary once again, until the exhausted and often badly injured suspect gave up the battle. Town councils were usually happy to approve the use of torture whenever courts requested it. And the pope's instruction not to kill the victim was not always helpful either. It was difficult to get an uncooperative suspect to confess without running the risk of incurring the subject's death.

Degrees of Torture

The process of using torture to obtain a confession was well standardized, especially where heresy was concerned. First, those accused would be given a chance to confess. If that failed, the prisoner would be taken as far as necessary through five levels, or degrees, of torture. The first degree was painless, physically at least; it consisted of showing the prisoner a variety of torture instruments. Sometimes it was necessary for the torturer to describe in great detail what each device did. More often, though, prisoners were able to determine the use of each instrument for themselves.

Simply seeing the devices convinced many people to confess to whatever the charges were, often regardless of whether they were truly guilty.

If the first degree failed, and it sometimes did, interrogators turned to the second degree. Typically this involved subjecting the victim to torture for up to a minute or so. In a grim perversion of Christianity, the time was measured by having the torturer recite a prayer while the pain was being inflicted. Those unwilling to confess after seeing the instruments of torture very often admitted guilt when the pain actually began. But should the second degree likewise fail, there were still three more degrees to go. The third degree—the phrase survives in modern English to indicate a period of intense questioning, often including violence—was much like the second degree but lasted longer. The fourth and fifth degrees added ever more fiendish punishments, some of which could culminate in significant blood loss, the breaking of bones, and the dislocation of shoulders and other joints. These degrees of torture were used mainly for those suspected of what an early twentieth-century historian called "atrocious and scandalous crimes."[22]

But even the fifth degree of torture was not sufficient to obtain a confession from every victim. Part of the reason was that a few prisoners, knowing that they were innocent, absolutely refused to admit to wrongdoing no matter how unspeakable the torments became. The other issue was that prisoners often were not told what specific charges they were facing. As a result, victims of torture sometimes had no idea what they were supposed to confess to. "Loosen me, Senores!, and tell me what I [must] say," cried a Spanish woman while being tortured for a crime she could not identify; "I do not know what I have done."[23] No one knows how many medieval Europeans never knew the charges against them, but no doubt the number is high.

WORDS IN CONTEXT

culpability: Guilt.

Confessions and the Innocent

The notion of torturing suspects to obtain a confession is problematic for several reasons, and all the more so because it was frequently used against people who had no idea what they were accused of. But perhaps the most

An unfortunate soul is subjected to the third degree of torture. He is stripped and an iron chain is pulled across his chest until it cuts through the flesh to scrape against his bones.

appalling part of these tortures was the fact that they were so often used against innocent people. People were suspected of heresy, witchcraft, and other crimes on the flimsiest of grounds: because someone in authority did not like them; because they were diseased, disfigured, or mentally challenged; or because some unfortunate neighbor, eager to bring his or her own torture to an end, identified them as fellow sorcerers or religious rebels. The merest hint of culpability, unfortunately, was usually enough to set the system of torture into motion. The interrogators, torturers, and other officials responsible for inflicting the pain wholeheartedly believed that they were doing God's work, especially where crimes such as witchcraft and heresy were concerned.

The fate of those who did confess at some point throughout the five degrees of torture varied. Some, especially those who were leaders in a heretical movement or those whose crimes were considered particularly

Ordeal by Combat

Perhaps the earliest ordeal to be widely used in medieval times was ordeal by combat, which was current in what is now Germany as early as the 700s. Ordeal by combat was most often used when two men quarreled over land, a contract, or some other legal issue. Court officials would assign the two men to engage in a swordfight. In essence, ordeal by combat was a state-sanctioned duel.

Ordeal by combat could last anywhere from a few minutes to several hours, depending on the skill and stamina of the combatants. It ended when one participant surrendered, knowing he was outclassed, or when one combatant was too badly injured to continue—or had been killed. The winner was awarded the victory in the lawsuit: He had clearly received the favor of God. The loser, in contrast, had been allowed to lose by God because his claim was false. The duel thus settled the case before the court.

Not all medieval Europeans accepted the ordeal by combat as an accurate indicator of the truth. A German law of the 1300s briefly eliminated the practice, noting that it could be difficult to tell whether a person had won the contest because God was on his side or because he was a more skilled swordsman. As a result of concerns like these, the process was occasionally modified to allow people to appoint someone to fight on their behalf. Still, the basic principle of the ordeal by combat remained in use till late in the medieval era.

heinous, were put to death as punishment for what they had done. Others were sentenced to more torture before being released. Still others were put in prison. Those who not only confessed but expressed sorrow for their actions might be set free with the admonition to adhere closely to the law—or to the Church's teachings—in the future. Indeed, for the more kind-hearted of Church officials, setting the one-time heretic free was often the best possible outcome of a heresy trial. An erring Christian had renounced a dangerous heresy and had returned to the fold, making it possible for the person's soul to go to heaven after death—an impossibility, as the Church saw it, for a heretic.

Torture, then, was used by medieval authorities in three very different ways. In addition to being used as punishment for people who had been found guilty of crimes, it was also used to determine whether a person was innocent or guilty and to encourage a prisoner to offer a confession for wrongdoing. While these uses may strike twenty-first-century Americans as harsh, even appalling, they are in some sense merely reflections of the medieval era. In a superstitious society where witchcraft was accepted as absolutely real, it is no surprise that trial by ordeal would flourish. And in a violent age where armies fought bloody battles on the slightest of pretexts, it is hardly a shock that violence would be seen as a perfectly acceptable way of getting a confession. The use of torture in the medieval world was entirely in keeping with the values and ideas of the time.

CHAPTER THREE

Medieval Prisons

The medieval justice system could choose from a broad array of possible punishments for those convicted of crimes. Torture, for instance, was used by every government throughout the Middle Ages. The death penalty was imposed, similarly, by essentially all medieval courts. Confiscation of property was common, as were fines; in England during the 800s, convicted rapists might be fined sixty shillings—an enormous amount for the time. Heretics could be forced to wear a yellow cross or be told to make a pilgrimage—a sacred journey to a place of spiritual significance, such as Jerusalem in the Middle East. And exile, or making a criminal leave the country, was widely used as punishment as well. Whether found guilty by an ecclesiastical court in fourteenth-century Portugal or by a secular judge in seventh-century Scotland, convicted criminals could expect one or more of these consequences as punishment for their activities.

Still, the defining experience common to virtually all medieval European criminals was not a specific punishment such as exile or torture. Instead, it was prison. All across the continent, suspected criminals were locked up while their guilt or innocence was determined. Those who were found guilty were imprisoned as well while they awaited torture, execution, or some other penalty. And for some prisoners, though by no means all, a prison sentence of weeks, months, or years was a main part of their punishment following conviction. Regardless of their crime, the nature of the accusations against them, or where and when they lived, few medieval Europeans who were caught up in the justice system avoided spending any time at all behind bars.

"Tomblike Enclosures"

Early medieval prisons were many things, but comfortable and pleasant were not among them. Quite a few of these prison cells were what would today be called dungeons. Small and stuffy, they were often in the lowest levels of castles or public buildings. Heavy doors, lockable from the outside, penned the prisoners in and kept fresh air out. The cells were freezing in the winter and could be sweltering in the heat of summer. With the exception of an occasional guard providing food or prosecutor demanding a confession, few visitors came to these dungeon cells, isolating the prisoner and causing psychological harm. One modern writer describes the typical prison cell of the Middle Ages as a "tomblike enclosure of stone or brick into which no ray of light ever penetrated and no human being ever set foot."[24]

WORDS IN CONTEXT

pilgrimage: Sacred journey to a holy place.

A restored dungeon in a medieval castle in what is now the Czech Republic provides a glimpse of the conditions prisoners were force to endure. Isolated and suffering from cold and lack of food, many never emerged alive from their underground cells.

Several other features made early medieval prisons even more repellent. One was chains, also known as irons. Though escape through a locked door of the cell was difficult, many prisoners were kept in heavy iron chains. The ends of the chains were fastened tightly to the wall or floor of the cell, then connected to the prisoner's ankles, wrists, or both. The chains severely restricted movement and sometimes cut into the prisoner's skin. William Marish, a noted outlaw of thirteenth-century England, was one of many captives kept in chains throughout his imprisonment. After being arrested for robbery and murder, Marish and his associates were sent to the Tower of London; according to the instructions given to their jailers, Marish and his men were to be "safely confined in the direst and most secure prison in that fortress, and so loaded with irons . . . that there could be no fear of their escape."[25]

Animal pests were another issue in the prisons of early medieval Europe. Able to squeeze themselves through astonishingly small spaces in the stone walls, rats were attracted to the cells by the prisoners' meals and body wastes. Sometimes they lurked in the shadows, coming out only when the prisoners were asleep and scurrying back to safety if they awoke; but some rats were quite aggressive, occasionally fighting prisoners for scraps of food. Other animals caused problems as well. One observer described German prisons of the late medieval period as "crawling with snakes and toads."[26] Fleas and other biting insects hid in the hay or straw that served as the prisoners' beds, making the captives' lives miserable. Body lice were almost impossible to get rid of once they infested a prisoner, and cockroaches crawled back and forth over the cell floor—and over the unfortunate captives as well.

> WORDS IN CONTEXT
>
> **dungeons: Small, cramped, and dark prison cells, usually with stone walls.**

Crowding, Food, and Death

Some prisoners' experiences in jail were made worse by being crammed together with a dozen other captives into a space designed for a few. Under these conditions, it could be impossible for a prisoner to lie or sit, and the overcrowding often led to arguments and fights. Then again,

Fleas, lice (pictured in this magnified image), and cockroaches made life miserable for captives held in medieval prisons. Scurrying rats and other creatures added to the horrors of imprisonment.

being kept in an isolated cell was not ideal either. Particularly difficult prisoners were often kept in solitary confinement where they saw no one but an occasional guard or soldier delivering food. In 1310, for instance, England's king Edward II placed a number of knights suspected of heresy in solitary confinement in the hope that they would confess their crimes. Though most of these men did not break under the stress of isolation and loneliness, the psychological strain of solitary confinement could be intense, and some people never fully recovered from the ordeal.

Food, or the lack of it, was a problem for prisoners, too. Most prisoners were given nothing to eat but bread and water—as one official describes it, "the bread of suffering and the water of tribulation"[27]—and not much of that. The bread, moreover, was likely to be stale or moldy and the water brackish. Prisoners with money, a minority of those in custody,

Escape

Escape from a medieval prison cell was possible, though not easy. Sometimes escape was accomplished through bribery. A prisoner with access to money might offer cash to a poorly paid guard, who would in turn purposely neglect to bolt the dungeon door all the way when he left that prisoner's cell. Alternatively, it might be done through guile. An unrestrained prisoner might complain of sudden illness, leading a guard to come into the cell to check what was going on. At that point the prisoner—healthy after all—might jump up, overpower the guard, and escape.

Most often, though, those who escaped had help from outside the prison. In 1322, for instance, a nobleman named Roger Mortimer was imprisoned inside the Tower of London after attempting to overthrow England's Edward II. Mortimer had important friends, however, and the following year they hatched a plot to release Mortimer. With the help of a tower official, who drugged most of the guards one evening, they made their way into the prison while the guards slept.

Cutting holes in the walls of Mortimer's cubicle, they spirited him out of his cell, over the roofs of two adjoining towers, and down to the nearby Thames River by means of a rope. It was a dramatic escape and an embarrassing one for the king. But Mortimer's freedom did not last. In 1330 he was recaptured, and this time he was sentenced to death.

could sometimes bribe their guards to bring them more food or food of a higher quality. This could also happen if a prisoner's friends or family were wealthy enough to pay for upgrades. Unfortunately, prosecutors often seized the property of prisoners before they were placed in their cells, and assisting a convicted or suspected criminal was frowned upon by most medieval Europeans. The result was that many prisoners went hungry, sometimes to the point of starvation.

Indeed, many prisoners died as a direct result of their confinement. Starvation was only one reason. Others died of exposure, particularly during the winter, due to a lack of sufficient clothing or blankets in unheated cells. Even heating a prison cell could lead to death, though; most heating in medieval Europe came from open fires that burned wood or charcoal, and if a fire began to spread it was usually impossible for a locked-in prisoner to escape. Still other prisoners died of disease, their immune systems weakened by poor food, extreme temperatures, and lack of exercise. And otherwise healthy prisoners might succumb to diseases brought in by fleas, rats, or other vermin. The unhygienic conditions and cramped quarters of the dungeons meant that prisoners were especially affected by viruses and germs, and death was common for those who became ill.

Noble Captives

Not all prison cells of the early Middle Ages were as awful as the dungeons where most prisoners were kept. In general, the dungeons were reserved for peasants and other members of the lower classes. Prisoners of the higher classes could expect better treatment: bigger and airier cells, no chains, even a set of rooms in a castle. This was especially true when they were held captive for political reasons. "His was an honorable confinement," writes historian Derek Wilson about Welsh rebel Gruffydd ap Llewelyn, who was arrested by English forces in 1241, taken to the Tower of London, and imprisoned in a suite of several rooms. "He enjoyed the company of his son, Owain, and a number of his friends and supporters."[28]

High-ranking prisoners of war were also subject to relatively gentle treatment. Knights, nobles, and other leaders of opposition armies were frequently held for ransom. English ruler Richard I, also known as Richard the Lionheart, was one example. In 1192, while returning from a Middle Eastern military campaign, Richard was captured by Austrian

Richard I of England was held in Dürnstein castle (pictured) after being captured in Austria in 1192. Imprisoned kings and nobles were often treated as honored guests until their captors obtained a ransom for their return.

forces and imprisoned in a castle called Dürnstein. The accommodations he was offered, like Gruffydd's in the Tower of London, were at least reasonably comfortable. "It was the tradition in the twelfth century to consider high-born prisoners as honored guests,"[29] writes historian David Boyle. Richard's captors had an incentive, moreover, to keep him in good condition; no one would pay a ransom for a king who was starving to death. In Richard's case, the plan worked. The English eventually delivered 65,000 pounds (29,484 kg) of silver to the Austrians in exchange for their king.

But being of noble birth was no guarantee that prison life would be easy. On the contrary, sometimes leaders treated political opponents from the ruling class more harshly than they would have treated common peasants or soldiers. This was especially the case during longstanding conflicts, when positions on both sides had hardened and angry feelings were common. Some castles were equipped with a special chamber, called an oubliette, for the purpose of imprisoning enemies, especially political prisoners. The oubliette was a cell with a hatch in the ceiling. Prisoners were lowered through the hatch on a rope, after which the opening was closed, leaving the prisoner in darkness and isolation. Sometimes the hatch was sealed, and the prisoner was left to die a lingering death. Even if the captors did occasionally lower food and water through the hole and eventually release the captive from the cell, the psychological effect on the prisoner was significant. Pembroke Castle in Wales was one of many medieval structures equipped with an oubliette.

WORDS IN CONTEXT

oubliette: Small prison cell with a single opening in the ceiling.

Prison Sentences

Today, prisons house two different kinds of people. They are used to house suspects, particularly those accused of serious or violent crimes, until they can be put on trial. And they are also used for convicted criminals, who may be sentenced to a period of days, months, or years in captivity. The first of these uses was a common purpose of prisons during the Middle Ages. Indeed, incarceration not only served to keep suspects away from innocent citizens but frequently functioned as a tool for determining guilt or innocence as well. Keeping people in prison under awful conditions, legal authorities believed, made them willing to do almost anything to get out, up to and including admitting guilt for crimes real or imagined. "Prisoners [are] habitually constrained to confession by the harshness of prison, the lack of beds, and the deficiency of food,"[30] a 1306 papal report noted approvingly.

In contrast, the second purpose—prisons as punishment for crimes—was much less commonly used in the Middle Ages. Until the end of the medieval era, it was relatively rare for thieves, heretics, or witches to be sentenced to spend a specified period of time in jail. Punishment typically consisted instead of torture, death, or another penalty such as exile or a fine. If a crime was serious enough that the criminal needed to be removed from the population, it was generally considered better to sentence the offender to death rather than risk having the same behavior repeated after the prison sentence ended. Nor, for the most part, did government and Church officials have the resources to keep people in prison for months or years, as is frequently done today. Since most public buildings had only a handful of jail cells, it made sense to move people in and out of them quickly.

Nonetheless, it was not unknown for early medieval Europeans to be sentenced to long terms in jail. People arrested for debt, in particular, were often given open-ended sentences in which they languished in prison until they came up with the money. Given that the debtors were imprisoned and unable to work, this was a difficult task at best; it was left to friends and relatives, many of them impoverished themselves, to pay off the debts and release the prisoners, and this often proved impossible. As a result, debtors often spent ten, twenty, or even thirty years in captivity—a solution which benefited neither the debtor, who paid with his or her freedom, nor the creditor, who never saw the money he or she was owed. Even so, jail terms such as these for debt were common across medieval Europe.

As the medieval era progressed, moreover, prison sentences became more commonly used to punish those convicted of crimes. Sometimes these were relatively short terms of, say, three or five years. Perhaps more often, though, the imprisonment was for life. In 1316, for example, an elderly woman in France was found guilty of heresy. As it happened, she was a repeat offender: Forty-eight years earlier she had been convicted of heretical thinking as well. Eager to be rid of her for good, the woman's accusers sentenced her to "perpetual imprisonment in chains."[31] That same decade, another mass trial of suspected heretics resulted in life terms for sixty-five unfortunate souls. If prisoners

Negotiating a Ransom

One of the best ways of obtaining money during the medieval period was to hold an opposition leader for ransom. The capture of a single high-born noble such as England's Richard the Lionheart could fill a treasury and provide funds for new military adventures. And when the prisoners were kings such as Richard—or John II of France, captured by the English in 1357—it was easy to obtain a huge payment in exchange for the captive's safe release.

For lower-ranking prisoners, however, captors often overestimated the ransom they could receive. Sometimes they thought a prisoner was more valuable to the other side than he actually was. Alternatively, they misjudged how much money the prisoner's government had. Whatever the reason, many noble prisoners throughout the Middle Ages languished for months or years while governments negotiated a ransom. Captured by English forces in 1335, for instance, Scotland's Earl of Murray spent five years as the subject of haggling between the two governments.

Over time, captors often reduced the ransom. But since it was clear that the prisoner was worth less than they originally believed, they moved the captive into less comfortable conditions. The Earl of Murray, for instance, began his imprisonment in a suite of rooms and ended it in chains. In some cases, it proved impossible to collect on any ransom at all. The Earl of Murray was eventually exchanged for an unransomed English prisoner captured by Scottish forces—a common ending when ransoms were not forthcoming.

could show that they had truly repented of their crimes, they might be set free sooner than expected. But there was no standard parole, probation, or expectation of early release in the justice systems of the Middle Ages.

Later Prisons

The increasing willingness to use prison sentences toward the end of the medieval period came about in part because of changes in prison construction and design, particularly in Italy. By the early 1300s cities such as Genoa and Venice were building prisons with much greater capacity than the typical fortress or courthouse could boast. As urban areas grew during this time, thanks largely to increasing prosperity resulting from higher levels of trade, civic and Church authorities saw an opportunity to streamline the prison system and make it more efficient. Specifically, they decided to replace the multiple prison cells scattered around a city with one larger building that could hold dozens of prisoners at once.

WORDS IN CONTEXT

irons: Metal chains used to limit prisoners' movements.

These prisons offered a variety of accommodations, from closely guarded cells in which prisoners remained chained most of the time to much looser living situations in which prisoners were allowed to roam the building and grounds very nearly at will. Where a prisoner was placed depended partly on the criminal's offense. Those who had committed more serious crimes typically lived under more tightly controlled conditions. Equally important, though, was the prisoner's rank and wealth. The richer and higher-status a person was, the more likely he or she was to be placed in airier, less closely watched quarters. "Better cells, better food, light, heating, bedding, etc., were normally for sale,"[32] writes historian Guy Geltner about later medieval prisons.

And certainly the accommodations at the upper end of this scale were a good deal less harsh than the castle prisons of the earlier Middle Ages had been. By modern standards, at least some prisoners were given a great deal of freedom. Indeed, according to Geltner, a few prisoners "left their cells to beg [for food and money], pursued their legal affairs, and attended family events."[33] Visitors were often welcome in late medieval prisons, too, including family members, priests, and doctors, among others. These changes did not make the prisons of the later Middle Ages comfortable places to live, but they certainly made life behind bars more bearable for those imprisoned at the time.

But the improvements at the end of the medieval period notwithstanding, a medieval prison was at best a miserable place to be. Whether prisoners were chained in unheated cells or allowed to move more or less at will through the prison complex, they were still prisoners. The vast majority of prisoners lived at the mercy of their guards. They ate poorly, shared their living quarters with rats and fleas, and rarely if ever received visitors. Unless they had been sentenced to a specific prison term, they never knew when, or whether, they would be released—and they could only imagine what might be in store for them afterward. Spending time in a medieval jail was a dreadful experience.

CHAPTER FOUR

Tortures and Torments

Medieval jails were appalling places. But for medieval criminals and suspected criminals who experienced torture as well as prison, incarceration was generally the easy part of the penalty. Time in a prison cell was usually preferable to medieval punishments that involved the infliction of physical pain. These tortures not only made up a large share of punishments for criminals during the medieval era but were also used to assist interrogators as they questioned suspected wrongdoers. Fiendish in their design and ghastly in their application, they are what most people think of today when they picture the punishments of the Middle Ages.

Some medieval tortures were designed to bring about the victim's death; capital punishment in the Middle Ages typically involved intensive torture with death the inevitable result. However, the bulk of medieval torture methods were not part of a death sentence. Though some of them could—and often did—eventually lead to the prisoner's death, the intent was not to kill but to simply inflict pain. These tortures varied, moreover, in how much pain and suffering they caused. At one end of the scale were tortures given for relatively minor offenses, which harmed victims but did not lead to disfigurement or any other permanent damage to the body. From there, however, tortures gradually increased to levels that ultimately encompassed mutilation and other permanent effects. Physically and psychologically, those who survived these torments were never the same again.

Branks, Stocks, and the Pillory

Those who were subjected to relatively mild torture as punishment were lucky. Yet even the mildest tortures of the Middle Ages were fairly harsh. A good example is the branks (or scold's bridle) which was developed toward the close of the medieval period. The branks were used on women who were accused of being scolds or gossips. The branks consisted of a metal headpiece which fit snugly around the skull, together with an attachment that extended into the mouth and flattened the tongue. Though the wearer of the bridle could still make noises, ordinary speech was out of the question—a fitting punishment, or so medieval authorities believed, for one whose words were offensive.

The scold's bridle was designed not just to keep the victim from speaking; it was also intended to humiliate. Some branks were shaped like the heads of animals. Others included bells that jingled as the wearer walked. These called attention to the scold wherever she went, guaranteeing that she would never escape notice. That provided an opportunity for townspeople who had been victimized by a scold to mock and insult her without needing to fear reprisal. For repeat offenders, the attachment that extended into the mouth could be covered with spikes that cut into the tongue, causing further pain and distress. The bridle was typically prescribed for no more than a few hours, since the device made eating impossible and drinking difficult; more than a day of use risked killing the wearer.

WORDS IN CONTEXT

pillory: Device that held a prisoner's hands and head in place.

Other punishments designed primarily to humiliate lawbreakers included the stocks and the pillory. The stocks were a set of wooden boards with holes for wrists and ankles. The prisoner's hands and feet were put through the holes and often chained together, holding the prisoner firmly in place. The pillory was much the same, except that the prisoner stood, and the holes were for the neck and the wrists rather than the wrists and the ankles. Both devices forced prisoners into uncomfortable and often painful positions. Exposed to the elements, the prisoners sweated under the hot sun in summer and shivered through cold in the winter.

As painful experiences go, being locked in the stocks was not in itself especially awful. But most stocks and pillories were located in town centers or village squares, so criminals imprisoned by the wooden boards were on public display. Often their fellow villagers threw rocks, rotten food, animal dung, and other items at them. When these objects found their target, they could break bones, knock out teeth, and damage the eyes. "Only the most innocuous transgressors could hope to get away with no more than a few black-and-blue marks and a couple of bumps," writes historian Robert Held. "Children's books, cinema, television, and the modern image industry generally . . . portray the stocks in humourous colours. . . . Reality was different."[34]

Nonetheless, by the standards of the Middle Ages the stocks and pillory, like the scold's bridle, were low-level penalties. They were reserved for those who had committed relatively minor offenses, such as petty

Two lawbreakers suffer the discomfort and humiliation of the stocks. To show contempt for their actions, villagers often threw rocks, rotten food, and animal dung at the prisoners.

theft, spreading malicious gossip, or taking part in a fistfight that caused no serious injuries. Depending on the severity of the offense and the offender's history, a criminal might spend anywhere from an hour to a day in the stocks or the pillory. The unfortunate prisoner would then be released, often bruised and battered and smelling of garbage, with an admonition to avoid crime in the foreseeable future. Assuming that no permanent damage was done by flying objects, victims would soon recover—and might even change their ways.

Flogging, Food, and Fingernails

A more serious form of torture, often combined with the pillory, was known as flogging. The prisoner was held captive in the pillory or tied to a post, the upper back bare and exposed. Men with whips would lash the victim's back as he or she stood unable to move. The whips were designed to inflict maximum pain. Some medieval whips included small metal hooks that tore the skin and dug into the prisoner's body as the whip raked across the back, but even without the metal, the speed of the whip as it traveled meant that the pain would be intense. Though most cuts or other wounds caused by a flogging eventually healed, a particularly severe beating could leave ugly scars and permanently damage muscles and joints.

> WORDS IN CONTEXT
>
> **flogging: Whipping.**

Binding, or tying a prisoner extremely tightly with ropes, was another torture that often left scars. Sometimes the prisoner was tied to a post, as with a flogging, and the ropes were tied around the prisoner's wrists, ankles, and torso. Other times the victim was not tied to an object, and the ropes covered only the wrists and hands. If the ropes were fastened tightly enough, the pain could be excruciating; and the discomfort only became worse if the ropes were gradually loosened and then tightened again. In some cases the torture was more than the victim could bear. "The cords eating into the swelling flesh caused such exquisite torture," writes a historian of a medieval Austrian priest accused of heresy, "that . . . he begged piteously to be taken out and burned."[35]

Keeping criminals and suspected wrongdoers awake for extended periods of time also was used as a torture during the Middle Ages. The human body is not designed to go without sleep for long; but during the Inquisition, interrogators working in teams often forced suspected heretics to remain awake for forty consecutive hours or even more. If they did fall asleep, they were shaken or beaten until they woke again. Lack of food was used as a torture, too, with captives being denied food or kept on starvation diets until they admitted wrongdoing or until their prescribed punishment was at an end. Alternatively, victims might be given only heavily salted foods and briny water.

Everyday items were often used in these tortures, too. Sliding small wedges under fingernails and toenails could produce excruciating pain without leaving many scars. A device called the heretic's fork, a length of metal or wood with two sets of prongs at opposite ends, could be placed between the victim's chest and chin with the prongs placed against the flesh; the fork made it almost impossible for the victim to shift position without being stabbed. Even smells were used to torment unfortunate suspects. "Victims might be made to inhale the fumes of onions and sulphur until they retched,"[36] notes Jonathan Kirsch. Virtually anything, in short, could be used to inflict torture.

Mutilation

More serious tortures involved the removal of body parts. The loss of a hand was particularly common. Medieval societies frequently forced the removal of a thief's right hand, for instance. During the 1100s England's Henry II went further, decreeing that thieves should lose not only their right hand but their right foot as well, and he extended the same punishment to murderers and arsonists. Sometimes the amputation was done with a saw; other times the tool used was a knife or an axe. If authorities were feeling merciful, they gave the prisoner plenty of alcohol to drink to numb the pain and cauterized the wound following the amputation—that is, they closed it with a red-hot iron to stop the bleeding and limit infection. If they were not feeling merciful they did neither.

Water Torture

A favorite torture of the Inquisition was pouring water into victims' mouths as they lay on their backs. As water filled the prisoner's stomach, it put heavy pressure on the heart and lungs, causing intense pain. But though this torture was designed to cause suffering, the real terror was not physical but psychological. The steady influx of water into the mouth and throat made victims feel exactly as if they were drowning.

There are good biological reasons for this response. "Even a small amount of water in the glottis [the opening to the windpipe] causes violent coughing," writes a modern expert, "initiating a fight-or-flight response, raising the heart and respiratory rate, and triggering desperate efforts to break free. The supply of oxygen available for basic metabolic functions is exhausted within seconds." A modification of this procedure, known as waterboarding, has been used in modern times to obtain information from suspected terrorists.

This torture was highly successful in getting prisoners to confess. Filling the victim with a gallon (3.8L) or more of water was often enough to convince even the most recalcitrant of prisoners to admit everything, whether the charges were true or not, just to make the agony end. And of course a confession, even a confession obtained under duress, justified the inquisitors' methods—or so the inquisitors believed—and made it clear to any critics that they were pursuing the right people.

Quoted in Cullen Murphy, *God's Jury*. Boston: Houghton Mifflin, 2010, p. 92.

Nor were extremities the only body parts removed as punishment. In the early 1300s, for example, the torture of a group of Templar knights included the extraction of teeth and fingernails. The loss of lips or other facial features was common as well. "If a woman during her husband's life commits adultery with another man," reads a British law from the early 1000s, "she is to lose her nose and her ears."[37] (There was no corresponding penalty for a male adulterer.) Tongs, sometimes known as Spanish spiders, were used for pulling off fingers, breasts, genitals, and chunks of flesh. To increase the pain, torturers often heated the tongs until the merest touch of the iron against the flesh produced agonizing burns as well.

The removal of eyes was also much favored, especially by those who punished heresy. In the early 1200s, for example, a man named Simon de Montfort carried out a particularly gruesome form of torture after capturing a French town held by heretics. "He assembled one hundred of [the town's] defenders," writes Kirsch, "and ordered his soldiers to blind them and hack off their noses and upper lips. Only one victim was permitted to keep an eye so he could lead the others to the nearest town."[38] The punishment was not new. In 1014 Basil II of Byzantium (present-day Istanbul, Turkey) did the same to Bulgarian soldiers captured at the Battle of Kleidion. Like Montfort, Basil allowed one man in every hundred to keep a single eye.

Stretching and Compression

Many medieval torture devices caused great—and frequently permanent—physical damage in other ways. Several of these stretched or pulled victims in horrifying ways. A contraption called the stivaletto, for example, consisted of wooden planks to which the legs were tied, immobilizing the victim. Then the torturer inserted metal wedges between the planks and the legs, forcing the legs into intolerable contortions. If the torture lasted long enough, it would eventually break bones, dig into the flesh, and pull joints out of position, making it impossible for the victim to walk normally ever again—and often damaging the legs so badly that walking became completely impossible. "The wedges lacerated flesh and crushed bone," reads a modern account, "sometimes so thoroughly that [bone] marrow gushed out and the legs were rendered useless."[39]

WORDS IN CONTEXT

strappado: Device that allowed prisoners to be lifted to the ceiling.

The head crusher (pictured) inflicted extreme pain and often permanent damage as it compressed the skull. The prisoner set his or her chin on the lower bar of the device. The screw was then turned, forcing the cap down to squeeze the head.

The strappado was another device that stretched the body. Interrogators tied a victim's wrists behind his or her back and fastened weights to the ankles. A rope was then attached to a pulley on the ceiling, with one end fastened to the prisoner's wrists. At regular intervals the torturer

Medieval Torturers

Not much is known about the people who served as torturers during the medieval period. The names of many of the clerics who served as inquisitors were recorded at the time—the Inquisition typically kept thorough records of its activities—but what drove priests and monks to fill this gruesome role is often far from clear. In turn, even the names of most secular torturers, let alone their motivations for taking the jobs, have been lost to history. There is some indication that the job of torturer might be handed down from father to son, much as a silversmith or carpenter might train his children to follow in his footsteps; still, how common this tradition was, no one knows.

In a violent society such as medieval Europe, many, or perhaps most, torturers saw their work as necessary but fundamentally commonplace—that is, little more than a job, one ranking alongside being a soldier, say, or a storekeeper. Still, that description may not cover all medieval torturers, particularly not those who took part in the Inquisition. Historian Jonathan Kirsch, for example, believes that at least some inquisitors were sadists at heart: They enjoyed inflicting pain on their helpless victims. The torture chamber, writes Kirsch, was "a theater of pain in which the victim was put on display for the entertainment of his or her persecutors."

Jonathan Kirsch, *The Grand Inquisitor's Manual*. New York: HarperCollins, 2008, p. 108.

would pull on the rope, hoisting the prisoner into the air. The movement often dislocated the shoulders and threatened to pull the arms completely out of their sockets, and the ankle weights put enormous pressure on the legs as well. To add to the agony of the strappado, the torturer could raise the prisoner almost to the ceiling and then suddenly release the rope, causing the victim to plummet several feet and then stop with a jerk. During the Middle Ages, the strappado's effectiveness in causing pain and winning confessions from heretics earned it the nickname "the queen of torments."[40]

Though the medieval world was quite fond of machines that stretched the body, it also had a variety of devices that smashed body parts. The thumbscrew, a small vise into which the victim's thumbs, fingers, or toes were placed, was perhaps the best known of these tools. The torturer slowly but surely tightened the thumbscrew to increase pressure on the body parts trapped inside it. If tightened enough, the device would ultimately crush these extremities altogether, breaking bones, destroying knuckles and other joints, and causing permanent damage to the hand or foot. Compared to a strappado or a stivaletto, thumbscrews were easy to build and to store, and they were highly efficient. "The returns in terms of agony inflicted in ratio to effort invested," Held observes dryly, "are . . . highly satisfactory, particularly where complex and costly equipment is wanting."[41]

WORDS IN CONTEXT

thumbscrew: Vise used to smash fingers and other extremities.

An even more diabolical squeezing machine was known simply as the head crusher. It was mainly used to extract confessions from heretics, witches, and other suspected criminals, though it could be applied as punishment to convicted criminals as well. The victim's head was placed in a vise that gradually compressed the skull. If a confession came soon enough, the prisoner suffered greatly but could avoid any permanent damage. Waiting even a few seconds too long, however, could result in the crushing of teeth, the forcing of eyes from their sockets, and more. A third squeezing device, the so-called Scavenger's Daughter, compressed not just the fingers or the head, but the entire body, resulting eventually in the fracturing of bones and sometimes the snapping or crushing of the spine. Though death was not the inevitable result, it was rare for a person to recover fully from being placed in one of these macabre machines.

Spikes and Piercing

Cutting or piercing the body was also a common torture during the Middle Ages. The so-called interrogation chair, for example, was a chair with back, seat, and armrests covered with spikes. The victim was stripped naked and strapped onto the chair. So finely sharpened were the spikes that no matter how lightly the victim sat, spikes would inevitably penetrate the flesh and cause great pain. Interrogators could add to the pain by beating the victim's chest, legs, and arms, thereby driving the sharpened spikes further into the prisoner's body. To make matters worse, the wounds often caused infections. In a society with rudimentary medical understanding and no knowledge of antibiotics, death was frequently the result.

In some instruments of torture, the piercing function was combined with squeezing or stretching. That was the case with an especially diabolical device called the knee splitter. The knee splitter was a large vise big enough to hold a knee, an elbow, or some other portion of an arm or a leg. However, the inside of the splitter was also equipped with spikes. Tightening the knee splitter not only compressed the bones, joints, and muscles, it also drove the spikes into the flesh. The result was an extremely painful torture which frequently destroyed or severely damaged the limbs to which it was applied. Those who experienced this torture were often left permanently crippled and dependent on others to stay alive.

Tortures were a standard part of punishment in medieval Europe. Whether trying to obtain a confession or looking for vengeance for crimes committed, medieval authorities believed themselves to be completely justified in inflicting as much pain and humiliation as they could—and in as ingenious a way as they could find. Like other aspects of medieval punishment, the emphasis on torture sprang directly

Finely sharpened spikes covered the back, seat, and armrests of the interrogation chair (opposite). To enhance the pain, victims were stripped of their clothes and strapped into the chair so that the spikes directly punctured the skin.

from the culture of Europe in the Middle Ages. "In village games," writes historian Barbara Tuchman, "players with hands tied behind them competed to kill a cat nailed to a post by battering it to death with their heads. . . . A pig enclosed in a wide pen was chased by men with clubs to the laughter of spectators as he ran squealing from blows until beaten lifeless."[42] For a society that accepted such behavior as commonplace and unremarkable, the torture of human beings is perhaps no surprise.

CHAPTER FIVE

Capital Punishment

The worst and most grotesque tortures of the Middle Ages were those which led up to the imposition of the death penalty. As authorities in the medieval period saw it, a person who deserved to be put to death should be killed in as brutal a manner as possible. While today most countries that still carry out the death penalty strive to do so humanely and painlessly, such considerations would have been completely alien to the judges and other leaders of medieval Europe. To them, part of the purpose of the death penalty was to make people suffer; thus, finding a supposedly painless method of execution would have seemed pointless. The creativity and cruelty of the medieval period were nowhere more visible than in the tortures that served as precursors to death.

The Rack and More

Many of the tortures leading to capital punishment were similar to those that did not necessarily bring about the victim's death, with the main difference being one of intensity rather than design. Chief among these was a stretching instrument known as the rack. Unlike the strappado, which was designed to cause extreme pain though not to kill or even necessarily to maim a victim, the main purpose of the rack was to quite literally pull a person to pieces. The victim would be tied on a table equipped with a winch, hands fastened over the head and feet fastened at the other end of the table. As the winch was wound, the body was stretched tighter and tighter, with predictable results. Torturers of the Middle Ages boasted of being able to extend the body of a typical victim by several inches—in some cases, by nearly a foot (31 cm).

The rack did indeed destroy the body. The tighter the winch was pulled, the greater the damage. The arms and legs quickly became dislocated, and the spinal column tore or snapped. Muscles and internal organs stretched to, and then past, their breaking points. Before long, writes historian Robert Held, "the interrogatee [victim] is maimed for life." In some circumstances, the torturer was content to stop there, especially if the victim was a suspected heretic or witch who was now, at last, ready to confess. More commonly, though, the torture continued. After just a few more turns of the winch, Held adds, the victim becomes "dismembered and paralysed, and gradually, over hours and days, the life functions cease one by one."[43]

Whipping, likewise, was not usually a form of capital punishment. Though it could result in brutal scars and great pain, it did not generally result in the victim's death. But one form of whipping, known as flaying, did exactly that. Flaying involved flogging the unfortunate prisoner thoroughly and violently with a whip designed to cut away the skin. Each time the whip landed it sliced another section of skin from the body, causing bleeding and eventually death. Victims "suffered under the scalpel-like blade" of the ends of the whip, writes historian Geoffrey Abbott. "Their skins were peeled away, strip by strip, [killing them] as their flesh was laid bloodily bare." Of all the methods of execution in use during the Middle Ages, Abbott argues, flaying was "one of the worst . . . ever devised by man."[44]

WORDS IN CONTEXT

flaying: Cutting away layers of skin.

Starving prisoners to death was a third method of execution that bore a strong resemblance to a torture—in this case, limiting the food a victim could eat. In 1200s England, for example, hardened criminals—those who were deemed incapable of reform—were sometimes sentenced to die of starvation. Typically they did receive small bits of bread from time to time, but not enough to live on, especially given that their water intake was severely limited as well. "They [shall] drink not the day they eat, nor eat the day they drink,"[45] reads a directive of the period. With insufficient calories and nutrients coming into the body, the prisoner

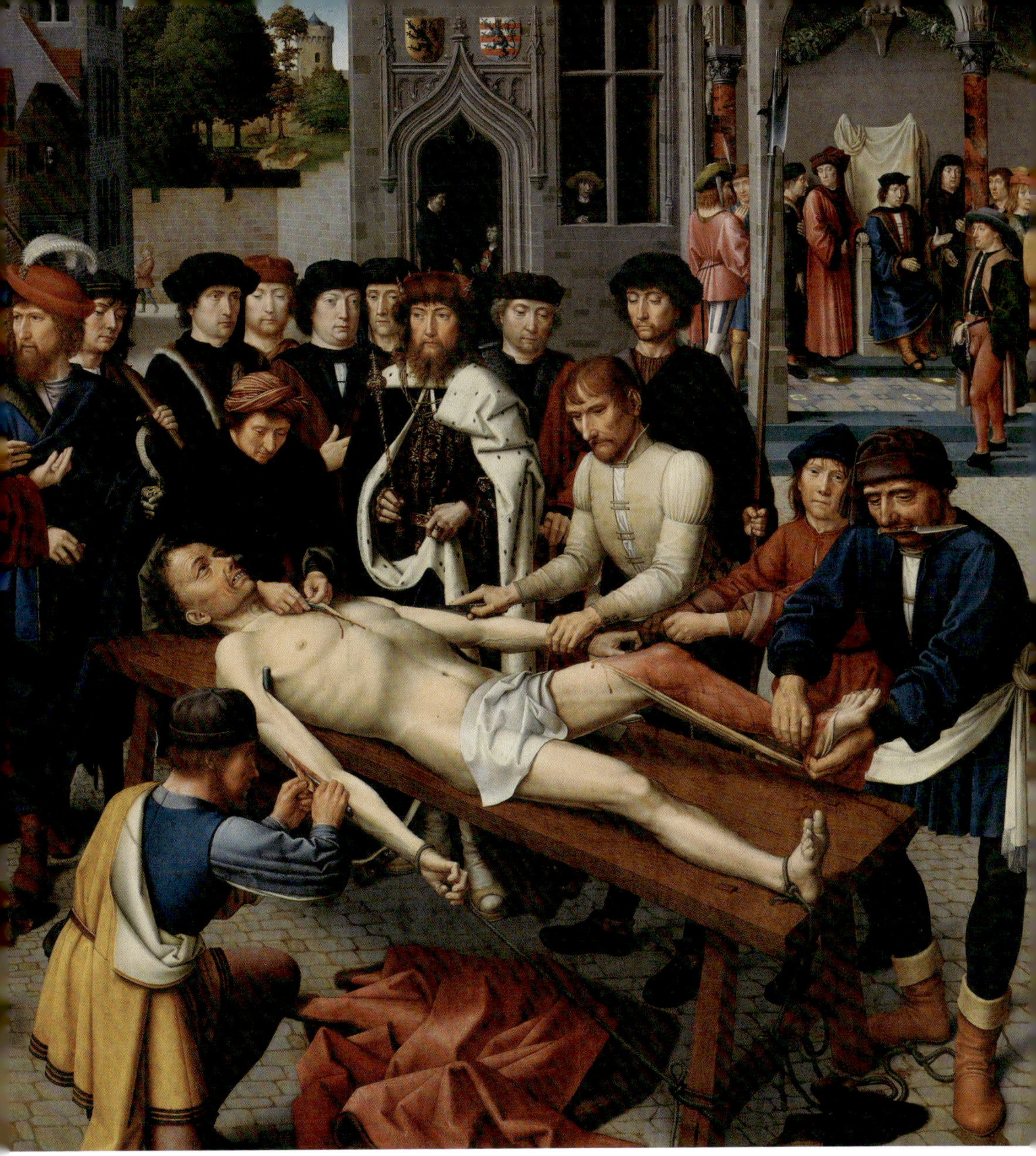

A gruesome form of execution—skinning, or flaying—is depicted in this painting by a fifteenth-century artist. Often this punishment involved a lengthy flogging with a whip designed to cut away the skin piece by piece until the victim died a most excruciating death.

could not survive more than several weeks. In other times and places, starvation was quicker and more direct; in parts of Spain, for example, prisoners sentenced to starve were locked in a tower with nothing to eat whatsoever.

The Fate of William Wallace

William Wallace was a Scottish patriot who was born in the 1270s. In 1297 he led a rebellion against the rule of English king Edward I, eventually managing to defeat the much stronger English army at a place called Stirling Bridge. He led several successful raids into England as well before finally leaving Scotland for continental Europe, where he tried to enlist support for the Scottish cause. In 1305, however, Wallace was captured by the English, tried at Westminster Abbey in London, and found guilty of treason. Part of his remarkably grim sentence ran as follows:

> For your robberies, homicides, and felonies . . . you shall be there hanged and drawn, and as an outlaw beheaded, and afterwards for your burning churches and relics your heart, liver, lungs and entrails from which your wicked thoughts came shall be burned, and finally, because your sedition, depredations, fires, and homicides were not only against the King, but against the people of England and Scotland, your head shall be placed on London Bridge in sight of both land and water travellers, and your quarters hung on gibbets [scaffolds] at Newcastle, Berwick, Stirling, and Perth, to the terror of all who pass by.

The story of Wallace is best known today as the basis for the 1996 movie *Braveheart.*

Quoted in Derek Wilson, *The Tower*. New York: Scribner, 1979, p. 35.

Painful Deaths

More often, though, capital punishments of the Middle Ages bore little resemblance to the tortures that were not designed to lead to death. In one particularly gruesome example of this type of torture, victims were turned upside down and tied in place with their legs spread apart. Two executioners then held the ends of a two-handled saw. Beginning between the legs, they slowly cut their way down through the stomach and chest until the victim was finally dead. "Owing to his inverted position, which assures ample oxygenation of the brain and impedes the general loss of blood," writes historian Robert Held, "the victim does not lose consciousness until the saw reaches the navel."[46] Until then, the prisoner could feel every stroke as the saw cut through flesh and bone—a horrific way to die.

Being burned alive was another example of an extremely grim and painful torture that led inevitably to death. Covered in tar, sulphur, or some other flammable material to speed the burning, the victim was tied to a stake and surrounded by straw and kindling which was then set ablaze. It usually did not take long before the victim's feet and legs were charred, but the victim often continued to live, usually in agony, until the fire had spread much further up the body. French military heroine Joan of Arc, who lived during the early 1400s, is just one of many thousands of Europeans who died in this manner during and shortly after the medieval era. Heretics and witches were especially often sentenced to die by fire.

WORDS IN CONTEXT

garrote: A device used to suffocate prisoners.

The garrote, a way of suffocating a prisoner, was also used extensively to kill victims during the medieval era. Mostly associated with Spain and Portugal, it remained a legal way of applying the death penalty in Spain until 1975. Prisoners to be garroted were tied tightly to a pole, and a metal collar was placed around their necks. At the rear of the collar was a screw which could be tightened, pulling the collar closer and closer to the throat. Executioners typically tightened the screw a little at a time, first making breathing difficult, then making it nearly impossible, and finally cutting off the prisoner's entire supply of air and causing death. A variation on the garrote added an iron point which pushed forward into the neck as the screw was moved, crushing the backbone in addition to blocking the airway.

Other common but appalling punishments were also designed to lead to death. Pressing was one of these. "A victim . . . lay on his back on the ground, arms and legs tied spread-eagle to stakes," writes author

Charles Panati, describing the procedure. "Across his chest rested a flat board. The torturer applied weights, one at a time, making breathing difficult, but taking measured care not to extinguish life too soon."[47] It could sometimes take several days before the victim actually died. Boiling alive, a quicker death than pressing, was probably more painful; it usually consisted of heating a cauldron of water over a fire and then dropping the prisoner into it. As the water grew ever warmer, it peeled the skin off the unfortunate victim and eventually cooked his or her internal organs. And a few medieval criminals suffered the terrifying fate of being buried alive. Sometimes this involved a coffin; more often, it did not. In one typical case, recorded in thirteenth-century France, a woman was lowered into a pit and then covered with boulders and dirt, causing her to suffocate.

Beheading and Hanging

Medieval societies did use several methods of capital punishment that offered the possibility of a quick and relatively painless death. One of these was beheading, which if accomplished with the aid of a sharp sword could end a prisoner's life in a matter of seconds. Indeed, some people who experienced this method of execution did die quickly. That was especially true of prisoners who were members of the nobility. In 1076, for instance, English ruler William the Conqueror arrested his enemy Waltheof, a high-born earl, and had him executed with a single strike of a sword. As long as the swordsman's aim was true and the prisoner did not flinch, it was possible to separate head from body in one smooth stroke.

But medieval executioners were more likely to use axes or knives to behead their prisoners, and these were not as reliable or as efficient as a well-honed sword. "Death did not always come quickly," writes Abbott. "The executioner was not noted for his expertise or his sobriety, and the axe he swung was heavy and unwieldy."[48] The fact that most beheadings were held in public, with large numbers of enthusiastic observers looking on, could put the executioner under added pressure, making him more likely to miss his target. The result was that death often took three, four, or more strokes with the blade, with painful consequences for the prisoner.

Hanging was another method of execution that could in theory be nearly pain-free. In a hanging, the executioner ties a rope around the neck of the condemned prisoner. As long as the prisoner's feet are resting on the ground, the rope is merely uncomfortable. But if the prisoner is suspended above the ground, whether from a tree or from a gallows—a wooden stand with a long arm from which the rope hangs—then the weight of the prisoner forces the rope to tighten, eventually suffocating the victim. There were two ways of causing death by hanging. The more painful and long-lasting was through suffocation. The more immediate came about by dropping the victim from a height, which could cause a broken neck and instant death when the rope reached its lowest point.

WORDS IN CONTEXT

gallows: Wooden arm from which a rope was suspended for hanging a person.

As with beheading, some fortunate prisoners died quickly when they were hanged. The vast majority, though, did not. They hung in the air, gasping for breath until their air supply was entirely extinguished—a process that could take many minutes. "Suffocation was torturously slow,"[49] writes Panati. That was especially true if the executioner decided to prolong the suffering by periodically lowering the victim to the ground, relieving pressure on the throat and permitting a more normal flow of air into the lungs. In an effort to add to the pain and make the hanging more of a spectacle for interested crowds, many medieval hangmen did exactly that. For these unfortunate victims, death, when it finally came, was undoubtedly a blessing.

Inhuman Tortures

But for every medieval prisoner who died quickly and easily, dozens more died in terrible agony—often in ways even more horrible than a slow hanging or a beheading by axe. Many prisoners were put to death on a device called the wheel, for instance. In this appalling torture, the victim was fastened to a wheel with an iron edge. The executioner then proceeded to

An executioner prepares to smash to bloody bits the body of a prisoner who has been fastened to the torture device known as the wheel. Once the job was done, the remaining flesh and bones were sometimes braided through the wheel's spokes.

literally break the person with an enormous hammer, smashing elbows, knees, hips, and other body parts while being careful not to cause death any sooner than necessary. The victim, one eyewitness reported, became "a sort of huge screaming puppet writhing in rivulets of blood, a puppet with four tentacles . . . of raw, slimy and shapeless flesh mixed up with splinters of smashed bones."[50] What was left of the victim was then braided through the wheel's spokes. If the victim was still alive, he or she was left outdoors for animals to scavenge.

The so-called Iron Maiden was scarcely any better. This device was a human-shaped container with two doors and spikes on the inside. The victim was placed inside the container, whereupon the doors were slowly closed. The results were predictable—and horrifying. "The very sharp points penetrated his arms, and his legs in several places, and his belly and chest," writes an observer who watched a criminal being put to death in one of these devices, "but not enough to kill him, and so he remained making great cry and lament for two days, after which he died."[51] As with the wheel, death would have been slow, lingering, and terrible.

If one medieval punishment stands out for its utter inhumanity, however, it might be neither the wheel nor the Iron Maiden, but rather a penalty known as drawing and quartering. In its most shocking form, the prisoner was first "drawn"—that is, cut open at the abdomen so torturers could pull out the victim's intestines. Remarkably, this did not immediately kill the prisoner, who was then forced to watch while the intestines were burned. Next came the quartering, in which each limb of the victim was tied to a different horse. The horses were then made to gallop away from one another, snapping the captive's muscles, bones, and joints as he or she was pulled simultaneously in four directions. In some cases the body was torn to pieces. If the prisoner still survived, he or she was usually beheaded at that juncture. Welsh prince David III was killed in this way by English officials in 1283.

A Public Spectacle

Capital punishment was designed not just to cause death and pain. It also frequently was a public spectacle. Throughout medieval Europe, especially toward the end of the Middle Ages, great crowds would gather to watch criminals be hanged, beheaded, or broken on the wheel. Witnessing a public execution was enjoyable for members of the crowd;

The Church and Capital Punishment

The medieval Church prided itself on not carrying out the death penalty on anyone who broke Church-related laws. "It was inappropriate for ecclesiastical officials to sully their hands with capital punishment," explains author Cullen Murphy. And for a religious organization dedicated, at least in theory, to feeding the hungry, helping the poor, and affirming the humanity of all people, it made sense that Church authorities would refuse to take human life for any crime at all.

The truth, however, was otherwise. The Church was not in fact opposed to capital punishment. Rather than put religious dissenters to death under its own auspices, the medieval Church simply gave convicted heretics over to secular authorities, who were happy to do the dirty work on the Church's behalf. Indeed, prisoners were handed over to secular officials as part of a ritual inside a church, usually on a Sunday following a service. "A throng would gather there," writes Murphy, "the ecclesiastical authorities, the secular magistrates, the public at large and the various sentences would be read out by the inquisitor. . . . To emphasize that the Church's hands were clean, the inquisitor would read a pro forma prayer, expressing hope that the condemned might somehow be spared—though there was in fact no hope of that."

The process of releasing convicted heretics to secular authorities allowed Church officials to keep up the pretense that they were compassionate and just, while at the same time getting what they really wanted—the deaths of their enemies, usually in grotesquely painful ways.

Cullen Murphy, *God's Jury*. Boston: Houghton Mifflin, 2012, p. 46.

several sources speak of the enthusiasm with which onlookers observed the suffering and death of convicted criminals. Indeed, the inhabitants of one French town purchased a prisoner doomed to be killed from a neighboring village so they could enjoy watching him die.

At the same time, authorities believed that public executions served as a deterrent to further crime. By watching while a person convicted of robbery, witchcraft, or treason was buried alive, drawn and quartered, or burned at the stake, the thinking went, onlookers would realize that they never wanted to experience such a punishment themselves. As a result, they would surely avoid committing serious crimes—or perhaps any crimes at all.

Modern historians generally believe, however, that public execution was no deterrence. Rather than dwindling in number, executions continued at a consistent rate throughout the Middle Ages. Part of the reason was the zeal of the Church and secular authorities for rooting out supposed heretics and witches, some of whom had done absolutely nothing wrong. Part of the reason was that medieval Europeans were able to rationalize their crimes, convincing themselves that they would not be caught and punished in such a horrendous fashion. Part of it, too, was that some peo-

Soldiers and other spectators watch as an unfortunate prisoner is drawn and quartered. His limbs are tied to four horses, each of which will pull in a different direction once his abdomen is sliced open.

ple had little choice in the matter but were driven to crime by forces such as poverty. In any case, the number of people arrested and executed for criminal activity was not affected by the prevalence of public executions.

Nor was the frequency of execution influenced by another grisly habit of the Middle Ages—the custom of displaying the corpses of those killed by the state. People killed by hanging, for instance, were sometimes left dangling for days or weeks as a warning to others. Similarly, severed heads were sometimes placed on the ends of spears and exhibited in marketplaces or other public venues. This practice was entirely in keeping with the violent tendencies of the medieval period. Unfortunately, like the custom of public execution, these warnings did little to limit the number of executions. Throughout the Middle Ages, a steady parade of heretics and robbers, thieves and rebels, witches and vagrants approached the stake, the gallows, or the Iron Maiden, there to suffer and die. The emphasis on not merely death, but blood, pain, and anguish, was one of the least pleasant—and to modern minds least understandable—aspects of the medieval era.

SOURCE NOTES

Introduction: The Middle Ages and Torture

1. Quoted in Barbara Tuchman, *A Distant Mirror*. New York: Knopf, 1978, p. 43.
2. Quoted in Jonathan Kirsch, *The Grand Inquisitor's Manual*. New York: HarperCollins, 2008, p. 2.
3. Quoted in Kirsch, *The Grand Inquisitor's Manual*, p. 58.
4. Quoted in Kirsch, *The Grand Inquisitor's Manual*, p. 48.

Chapter One: Crime in the Middle Ages

5. Tuchman, *A Distant Mirror*, p. 240.
6. Joyce Lee Malcolm, *Guns and Violence*. Cambridge, MA: Harvard University Press, 2002, p. 31.
7. Quoted in Noel James Menuge, ed., *Medieval Women and the Law*. Woodbridge, UK: Boydell, 2000, p. 133.
8. Quoted in Trevor Dean, *Crime and Justice in Late Medieval Italy*. Cambridge: Cambridge University Press, 2007, p. 198.
9. Quoted in Charles W. Eliot, ed., *Chronicle and Romance*. New York: P.F. Collier, 1910, p. 78.
10. Quoted in Ernest W. Pettifer, *Punishments of Former Days*. London: Waterside, 1992, p. 132.
11. Quoted in Kirsch, *The Grand Inquisitor's Manual*, p. 144.
12. Quoted in Kirsch, *The Grand Inquisitor's Manual*, p. 150.
13. Norman Cantor, ed., *The Encyclopedia of the Middle Ages*. New York: Viking, 1999, p. 445.
14. Quoted in Cullen Murphy, *God's Jury*. Boston: Houghton Mifflin, 2012, p. 25.
15. Quoted in Kirsch, *The Grand Inquisitor's Manual*, p. 20.
16. Quoted in Murphy, *God's Jury*, p. 31.
17. Kirsch, *The Grand Inquisitor's Manual*, p. 11.

Chapter Two: Ordeals and Confessions

18. Quoted in Oliver J. Thatcher, ed., *The Library of Original Sources,* vol. 4. Milwaukee: University Research Extension, 1907, p. 310.
19. Kirsch, *The Grand Inquisitor's Manual*, p. 95.
20. Quoted in Kirsch, *The Grand Inquisitor's Manual*, p. 94.
21. Quoted in Edward Peters, *Torture*. New York: Basil Blackwell, 1985, p. 55.
22. George Zurcher, *The Apple of Discord*. Buffalo, NY: Apple of Discord, 1905, p. 411.
23. Quoted in Murphy, *God's Jury*, p. 89.

Chapter Three: Medieval Prisons

24. Kirsch, *The Grand Inquisitor's Manual*, p. 99.
25. Quoted in Derek Wilson, *The Tower*. New York: Scribner, 1979, p. 11.
26. Quoted in Guy Geltner, *The Medieval Prison: A Social History*. Princeton, NJ: Princeton University Press, 2008, p. 97.
27. Quoted in Kirsch, *The Grand Inquisitor's Manual*, p. 99.
28. Wilson, *The Tower*, p. 27.
29. David Boyle, *The Troubadour's Song: The Capture and Ransom of Richard the Lionheart*. New York: Walker, 2005, p. 161.
30. Quoted in Kirsch, *The Grand Inquisitor's Manual*, p. 99.
31. Quoted in Kirsch, *The Grand Inquisitor's Manual*, p. 78.
32. Guy Geltner, "Medieval Prisons: Between Myth and Reality, Hell and Purgatory," *History Compass 4*, 2006, p. 4.
33. Geltner, "Medieval Prisons," p. 3.

Chapter Four: Tortures and Torments

34. Robert Held, *Inquisition*. Florence, Italy: Qua d'Arno, 1985, p. 66.
35. Quoted in Kirsch, *The Grand Inquisitor's Manual*, p. 107.
36. Kirsch, *The Grand Inquisitor's Manual*, p. 108.
37. Quoted in Robert Lacey and Danny Danziger, *The Year 1000*. Boston: Little, Brown, 1999, p. 171.
38. Kirsch, *The Grand Inquisitor's Manual*, p. 49.

39. Rosemary Ellen Guiley, *The Encyclopedia of Witches, Witchcraft, and Wicca*, 3rd ed. New York: Facts On File, 2008, p. 348.
40. Quoted in Kirsch, *The Grand Inquisitor's Manual*, p. 106.
41. Held, *Inquisition*, p. 92.
42. Tuchman, *A Distant Mirror*, p. 135.

Chapter Five: Capital Punishment

43. Held, *Inquisition*, p. 90.
44. Geoffrey Abbott, *Execution*. New York: St. Martin's, 2005, p. 113.
45. Quoted in Abbott, *Execution*, p. 232.
46. Held, *Inquisition*, p. 46.
47. Charles Panati, *Panati's Extraordinary Endings of Practically Everything and Everybody*. New York: Harper and Row, 1989, p. 141.
48. Abbott, *Execution*, p. 13.
49. Panati, *Panati's Extraordinary Endings of Practically Everything and Everybody*, p. 145.
50. Quoted in Held, *Inquisition*, p. 42.
51. Quoted in Held, *Inquisition*, p. 26.

FOR FURTHER RESEARCH

Books

William Andrews, *Medieval Punishments: An Illustrated History of Torture*. New York: Skyhorse, 2013.

Warren C. Brown, *Violence in Medieval Europe*. London: Routledge, 2010.

Mark P. Donnelly and Daniel Diehl, *The Big Book of Pain: Torture and Punishment Through History*. New York: History Press, 2012.

Ian Mortimer, *The Time Traveler's Guide to Medieval England: A Handbook for Visitors to the Fourteenth Century*. New York: Touchstone, 2011.

Cullen Murphy, *God's Jury*. Boston: Houghton Mifflin Harcourt, 2012.

Internet Sources

Fordham University, "Ordeal of Boiling Water," Medieval Sourcebook. www.fordham.edu/Halsall/source/water-ordeal.html. A primary source regarding the medieval ordeal by water.

Guy Geltner, "Medieval Prisons," Academia.edu. www.academia.edu/707904/Medieval_Prisons_Between_Myth_and_Reality_Hell_and_Purgatory. An article about prisons and prison life in the Middle Ages, especially in the later medieval era.

Historical Torture Museum, "Instruments Gallery." www.torturamuseum.com/instruments.html. Part of the website of a traveling museum exhibit on torture. Includes pictures and text about various torture methods and the role of torture in medieval society.

Medieval Times and Castles. www.medievality.com. Includes information on tortures and punishments in general and specific tortures as well.

Medieval Warfare, "Medieval Torture." www.medievalwarfare.info. Describes some of the specific tortures used in the Middle Ages along with the background on punishment at the time.

INDEX

Note: Boldface page numbers indicate illustrations.

Abbott, Geoffrey, 58, 62
accusations
  accused not told about, 28
  of adultery, 23, 24
  reasons for, 29
adultery
  accusations of, 23, 24
  punishments for women, 49–50
Alexander III (pope), 8
amputations, 48–50
animal pests, 34, **35**
appeals, 21
armed robbery, 11
arson, defined, 11

Barthe, Angela de la, 16
Basil II (of Byzantium), 50
beggars, 12–13
beheadings, 62–63
Bernabo (ruler in Italy), 10
Bible and ordeals, 22–23
bindings, 47
boiling alive, 62
Book of Numbers (Bible), 22–23
Boyle, David, 38
branding, 18
branks, 45
Braveheart (movie), 60
brawls, 11, 14, 34, 47
burglary, 11–12
burning alive, 7, 61
burying alive, 62

capital punishment
  Church and, 66
  as deterrent, 67–68
  methods used
    beheading, 62–63
    boiling alive, 62
    burning alive, 7, 61
    burying alive, 62
    drawing and quartering, 65, 67
    flaying, 58, 59
    hanging, 63
    Iron Maiden, 65
    rack, 57–58
    sawing while inverted, 60–61
    starvation, 58–59
    suffocation, 61–62, 63
    wheel, 63–65, 64
    withholding water, 58
  purposeful brutality of, 44, 57
chains, 34
Christianity. *See* Church, The
Church, The
  buildings as sanctuaries, 18
  capital punishment and, 66
  ecclesiastical courts, 21, 22
  heresy and, 19–20
  prayers used by torturer, 28
  violence and, 27
  water as symbol in, 25
  witchcraft and, 14–16, 19
  See also Inquisition
Clement V (pope), 6–7
coin clipping, 15
compassion, attitude toward, 8–9
compression devices, **51,** 53, 54
confessions
  as corrobation of presumed guilt, 25
  of heresy
    freedom after, 30–31
    importance of, 25

methods used to obtain, 22, 27, 35, 39, 47, 48, 49
obtaining
by incarceration, 35, 39
by torture, 22, 27–28
confiscation of property, 32
corpses, display of, 67
court systems, 21–22
crimes
capital punishment as deterrent to, 67–68
common
armed robbery, 11
brawls/fistfights, 11, 14, 34, 47
burglary, 11–12
coin clipping, 15
creation of public nuisances, 14
debt, 12
gossiping, 45, 47
heresy, 19–20
petty theft, 12, 13, 46–47
rape, 11
treason, 13–14
vagrancy, 12–13
violent, 10–11
witchcraft, 14–19, 17
reasons for making acts, 10
crushing devices, **51,** 53, 54
culpability, defined, 28
Cunigunde (queen of Luxembourg), 24

David III (prince in Wales), 65
death penalty. *See* capital punishment
debt, 12, 40
DeMolay, Jacques, 6–7
devil and witchcraft, 14–16
devil's mark, 16
disturbances of the peace, 14
drawing and quartering, 65, **67**
dungeons, **33**, 33–34, 37
Dürnstein castle, 38, **38**

ecclesiastical, defined, 22
Edward I (king of England), 15, 60
Edward II (king of England), 35, 36
England, **8**, 32, 58
entertainment, punishments as
beheadings and hangings, 62–63
branks, pillories and stocks, 45–47, 46
deterrence purpose of, 67–68
drawing and quartering, 67
popularity of, 65–66, 67
for the torturer, 52
Europe, map of medieval, **8**
executions. *See* capital punishment
exile, 32

familiars, 16
fifth degree of torture, 28
fines, 32
fire, 23–24, 61
first degree of torture, 27–28
fistfights, 11, 14, 34, 47
flayings, 58, **59**
flogging, 47, 58
food
in prisons, 34, 35–37
starvation
as method of execution, 58–59
as punishment, 48
as reason for theft, 12, 13
fourth degree of torture, 28

gallows, defined, 63
garrotes, 61
Geltner, Guy, 42
Genoa, 42
Germany, 30
Gies, Frances, 18
Gies, Joseph, 18
gossips/scolds, 14, 45, 47
Gregory IX (pope), 19
Gruffydd ap Llewelyn, 37
Gui, Bernard, 26
guilt
determination of, by ordeals, 23–25

presumption of, 17, 20, 22
prison conditions and admission of, 39
response to pain and, 22
See also confessions

hangings, 63
head crushers, **51,** 53
Held, Robert, 46, 53, 58, 61
Henry II (king of England), 14, 48
heresy
confessions
freedom after, 30–31
importance of, 25
methods used to obtain, 22, 27, 35, 47, 48
presumption of guilt, 20, 22
punishments for, 32
death, 29–30, 61
incarceration, 40–41
mutilation, 50
reasons for charges of, 19, 29
secular authorities and, 66
seriousness of, 19–20
See also Inquisition
heretic's fork, 48
homicide, 10–11
humiliation as punishment, 45–47, **46**

incarceration. *See* prisons
Inquisition
clerics as torturers, 52
described, 20
methods used, 48
textbook for, 26
Inquisitor's Manual, An (Gui), 26
insects, 34, **35**
interrogation chairs, 54, **55**
Iron Maidens, 65
irons (chains), 34, 42

Joan of Arc, 61
John II (king of France), 41

Kirsch, Jonathan
on admissions of heresy, 25
on Inquisition, 20
on punishment as entertainment, 52
on Simon de Montfort, 50
on use of ordinary items for torture, 48
knee splitters, 54
Knights Templars, 6–7, 49

lepers, 12–13

Malcolm, Joyce Lee, 10–11
Maleta, 11–12
Marish, William, 34
mercy, attitude toward, 8–9
Middle Ages, time span of, 7
Montfort, Simon de, 50
Mortimer, Roger, 36
murder, 10–11
Murphy, Cullen, 66
Murray, Earl of, 41
mutilation, 48–50

nobility
prison conditions for, 38, 42
ransoming of, 37–39, 41

On the Method, Practice, and Procedure Used in Seeking Out and Interrogating Heretics, Their Believers, and Accomplices (Gui), 26
ordeals
biblical precedent for, 22–23
by combat, 30
defined, 25
by fire, 23–24
pain-guilt correlation, 22
purpose of, 22
by water, 24–25, 49
oubliette, defined, 39

pain and guilt, 22

Panati, Charles, 61–62, 63
Pembroke Castle, 39
petty theft, 12, **13,** 46–47
Philip the Fair (king of France), 6–7
piercing devices, 54, **55**
pilgrimages, 32, 33
pillories, 45–46, 47
poker test, 23–24
political prisoners, 37–39, **38,** 41
poverty, 12
prayers, 28
pressing, 61–62
prisoner exchanges, 41
prisons
  conditions in
    admissions of guilt and, 39
    dungeons, 33, 33–34, 37
    food, 34, 35–37
    to force confessions, 39
    larger, newer prisons, 42–43
    for nobility or political prisoners, 37–39, 38, 41, 42
  death during confinement, 37
  debtors in, 40
  escape from, 36
  overcrowding vs. solitary confinement, 34–35
  for punishment of convicted, 40–41
property, confiscation of, 32
public punishments
  humiliation and, 45–47, 46
  See also entertainment, punishments as
punishments. *See* capital punishment; torture

queens of torment (strappados), 50, 51–53, 57

racks, 57–58
ransoms, 37–39, 41
rape, 11
recant, defined, 7
repentance, 40–41
revolts, 14
Richard I (Richard the Lionheart, king of England), 14, 37–39, **38,** 41
robbery, armed, 11
ruthlessness, defined, 9

sanctuary, right of, 18
Satan and witchcraft, 14–16
sawing while inverted, 60–61
Scavenger's Daughters, 53
scold's bridles, 45
scolds/gossips, 14
Scotland, **8**, 60
second degree of torture, 28
secular, defined, 19
sentences, 29–31, 32
  See also capital punishment
sleep deprivation, 48
solitary confinement, 35
sorcery. *See* witchcraft
Spain, **8**, 59, 61
Spanish spiders, 50
starvation
  as method of execution, 58–59
  as punishment, 48
  as reason for theft, 12, 13
stivalettos, 50
stocks, 45–46, **46**
strappados, 50, 51–53, 57
stretching devices, 50–53
suffocation, 61–62, 63
suspects, incarceration of, 39

Templars, 6–7, 49
theft, 11–12, **13**
third degree of torture, 28, **29**
thumbscrews, 53
torture
  degrees of, 27–28, 29
  humiliation and, 45–47, 46
  methods used

mutilation, 48
not resulting in permanent damage, 45–48, 46
piercing devices, 54, 55
stretching and compression, 50–53, 51, 54, 57
presumption of guilt, 22
torturers, 52
Tower of London, 34, 36, 37
treason, 13–14
Tuchman, Barbara, 10, 56
Tyler, Wat, 14

vagrancy, 12–13
Venice, 42
violence
Church officials and, 27
crimes of, 10–11
general societal level of, 31, 56

Wallace, William, 60
water
as method of torture, 24–25, 49
as symbol, 25
withholding, as method of execution, 58
waterboarding, 49
wheels (torture devices), 63–65, **64**
whippings, 47, 58
William the Conqueror, 24, 62
William the Lion, 14
Wilson, Derek, 37
witchcraft
burning alive, 61
Christianity and, 14–16, 19
presumption of guilt, 17
prosecutions for, 16–18, 17
wizardry. *See* witchcraft
women
adultery and, 23, 49–50
gossips/scolds, 14, 45, 47
rape of, 11

PICTURE CREDITS

Cover: Inquisition. Instrument of torture. Wheel of Fortune. Photo © Tarker/The Bridgeman Art Library

Maury Aaseng: 8

© amanaimages/Corbis: 38

AP Images: 51

© Corbis: 67

© Charles & Josette Lenars/Corbis: 55

© Dr. David Phillips/Visuals Unlimited/Corbis: 35

© Tarker/Corbis: 64

Thinkstock Images: 4, 5, 33

Ms 680/1389 Men stealing wheat, from 'The Fables of Bidpai', c.1480 (w/c on paper), German School, (15th century)/Musee Conde, Chantilly, France/Giraudon/The Bridgeman Art Library: 13

Woman on a Ducking Stool, Accused of Witchcraft, illustration from a collection of chapbooks on esoterica (woodcut) (later colouration), English School / Private Collection/The Stapleton Collection/The Bridgeman Art Library: 17

F.39r Conjugal Law, an adulterous wife appearing in court, from 'Justiniani in Fortiatum' (vellum), French School, (14th century)/ Biblioteca Monasterio del Escorial, Madrid, Spain/The Bridgeman Art Library: 23

Third Degree of Torture of the Inquisition, engraved by L.C. Stadler, pub. by Cadell & Davies, London, c.1813 (coloured engraving), English School, (19th century)/Private Collection/The Stapleton Collection/The Bridgeman Art Library: 29

Two Men in Stocks (oil on panel), German School, (15th century)/The Barnes Foundation, Philadelphia, Pennsylvania, USA/The Bridgeman Art Library: 46

The Flaying of Sisamnes, 1498 (oil on panel), David, Gerard (c.1460–1523)/Groeningemuseum, Bruges, Belgium/© Lukas—Art in Flanders VZW/The Bridgeman Art Library: 59

ABOUT THE AUTHOR

Stephen Currie has written many books for ReferencePoint Press, including *The Black Death, The Renaissance,* and *Medieval Castles.* He has also written educational materials and taught at levels ranging from kindergarten to college. He lives in New York State.